Abraham Lincoln and His Era

Using the American Memory Project to Teach with Primary Sources

Bobbi Ireland

A Teacher Ideas Press Book

LIBRARIES UNLIMITED
An Imprint of ABC-CLIO, LLC

A B C · C L I O

Santa Barbara, California • Denver, Colorado • Oxford, England

Copyright 2010 by Libraries Unlimited

All rights reserved. No part of this publication may be reproduced,
stored in a retrieval system, or transmitted, in any form or by any
means, electronic, mechanical, photocopying, recording, or otherwise,
except for the inclusion of brief quotations in a review or reproducibles,
which may be copied for classroom and educational programs only, without prior
permission in writing from the publisher.

Library of Congress Cataloging-in-Publication Data
Ireland, Bobbi.
  Abraham Lincoln and his era : using the American memory project to teach with primary sources / Bobbi Ireland.
       p. cm.
  ISBN 978-1-59158-902-0 (hard copy : alk. paper) — ISBN 978-1-59158-903-7 (ebook)
  1. Lincoln, Abraham, 1809–1865—Study and teaching. 2. Lincoln, Abraham, 1809–1865—Study and teaching—Audio-visual aids. 3. Lincoln, Abraham, 1809–1865—Sources. 4. United States—History—Civil War, 1861–1865—Study and teaching. 5. United States—History—Civil War, 1861–1865—Study and teaching—Audio-visual aids. 6. United States—History—Civil War, 1861–1865—Sources. 7. Library of Congress. National Digital Library Program. I. Title.
  E457.I74   2010
  973.7092—dc22   2009038498

ISBN: 978-1-59158-902-0
EISBN: 978-1-59158-903-7

14 13 12 11 10   1 2 3 4 5

This book is also available on the World Wide Web as an eBook.
Visit http://www.abc-clio.com for details.

ABC-CLIO, LLC
130 Cremona Drive, P.O. Box 1911
Santa Barbara, California 93116–1911

This book is printed on acid-free paper ∞

Manufactured in the United States of America

McRel 4th Edition Standards and Benchmarks. Copyright 2009. Reprinted with permission from *Content Knowledge: A Compendium of Standards and Benchmarks for K-12 Education*, 4th ed. www.mcrel.org/standards-benchmarks/ All rights reserved.

Contents

Chapter 1: What Are Primary Sources and How Do I Use Them in Class? 1
   Differentiated Instruction 2

Chapter 2: Lesson Plans Analyzing Primary Sources with Document Analysis Tools 5
   Letter from Justin Butterfield to Abraham Lincoln 5
   Bill to Abolish Slavery 9
   Speech Regarding the Mexican War 12

Chapter 3: Lesson Plans Using Rubrics to Evaluate Students' Performance 15
   Letter to Elihu B. Washburne 15
   Letters Between Abraham Lincoln and Stephen Douglas 20
   Letter from Joseph Medill 24
   Popular Sovereignty 28
   Congratulation Letters 32
   Letter from Julia Matie 36
   Letter Written by Grace Bedell 40
   Abraham Lincoln's First Inaugural Address 44
   Letter by Mrs. Luther Fowler 48
   Emancipation Proclamation 52
   Letter from Ulysses S. Grant about the First African American Troops 56
   Memo Written by Abraham Lincoln to His Cabinet 60
   Eyewitness Account of President Lincoln's Assassination 64

Chapter 4: Lesson Plans Incorporating the Arts and Humanities in Primary Sources 69
   Poem Written by Abraham Lincoln 69
   Certificate of Membership Given to Abraham Lincoln 73
   Photographs of Abraham Lincoln 77
   Painting by Thomas Nast 81
   Painting Showing the Assassination of President Lincoln 85
   Reward Posters 89
   Iron Casts Made of Abraham Lincoln's Hands 93

Appendix: Analysis Tools 97
   Cartoon 97
   Letter 99
   Map 101
   Photo: The More You Look, the More You See 103
   Motion Picture 105
   Poem 107
   Poster 109
   Photo: Put Yourself in the Picture 111
   Sheet Music 113

Storyboard 115
Sound Recording 117
Written Document 119
Photo: ABC 121

Bibliography 123
Index 125

CHAPTER 1

What Are Primary Sources and How Do I Use Them in Class?

A primary source is generally someone's firsthand view of an actual event. It is a piece of paper, art, video, or recording of an historical event. A secondary source is made from someone else's information. Imagine holding an actual copy of a letter written to Abraham Lincoln congratulating him on his election. What would it be like to hear the voice of a real former slave? The Library of Congress makes the above possible. According to the Library of Congress, its mission is "to make its resources available and useful to the Congress and the American people and to sustain and preserve a universal collection of knowledge and creativity for future generations." Teaching with primary sources is a wonderful opportunity for both teachers and students. These sources contain small parts of history. Students have to make inferences in order to complete activities. Students who have used primary sources gain a new sense of empathy for others and remember the actual historical event and link their personal feelings to it.

The Library of Congress is the largest library in the world, with more than 530 miles of bookshelves (Rich). The library collects not only books but also maps, audio and video recordings, photographs, and other printed materials. Anyone with an Internet connection can use the primary sources at the Library of Congress.

This book provides lesson plans to use in the classroom that utilize some of the primary sources in the Library of Congress at http://www.loc.gov. The lesson plans in this book are categorized into written documents and arts and humanities. Rubrics are included for the activities that are not analyses. Analysis tools are found in the appendix. These tools can be used with any primary source. Teachers are encouraged to use this book as a springboard to create lesson plans, rubrics, and analysis tools to meet their individual needs. Each lesson is cross-curricular and can be incorporated into many areas of study. When teaching students about Abraham Lincoln, most teachers use a textbook. How much more would students get from the lesson if they could actually hold a copy of handwritten history, such as a handwritten note, a photograph, or a newspaper clipping?

Using primary sources in the classroom is easy. Take some time to learn about the Library of Congress Web site at http://www.loc.gov. There is information placed throughout the site. Primary sources are found in Digital Collections and Exhibits. Allow adequate time to explore find out what the library has to offer and to explore all the areas of the site. Think of an era or a time frame that is interesting. Look for specific items that fit into an interest. Remember, primary sources can be newspaper clippings, posters, notes, memos, video or audio recordings, photographs, sheet music/songs, and much more. On the Library of Congress Web site, there is a section created for teachers called Tools for Teachers. It houses information like interesting things to look for, activity sheets, and lesson plans.

The lesson plans in this book utilize the American Memory collection. This collection is arranged by criteria such as alphabetical, size, categories, season/holiday, place, date, theme/event, and miscellaneous. Many think this collection is set up like an old attic. Think of all the items being stored in big boxes. During research, search through the saved "boxes" to find exactly what is needed. After a search is made and results are shown, click on the gallery view in order to see the primary sources. The other option is to see the name of the source. The sources are much easier to find when they are seen. When an image needs to be captured from the Web site, right click on the image and select "save picture as." Save the image on the computer in the preferred location. When the image is saved, it can be brought up as a document or multimedia presentation. When an audio or movie file needs to be captured from the Web site, right click on the link to the clip, and then left click on "save target as." Name and save the clip to the preferred location. Make sure to save the clip in the correct file format for the capacity that it will be used. When a primary source is found, save it or write down the title of the source so it can be found again. The Library of Congress Web site contains many "temporary" pages. This means that the pages that are visited are made at that time. For example, if it took five clicks to find a particular image and it is bookmarked, it really won't be saved. When the bookmarked address is used, the page won't build. When the primary source page is located, right click on the page other than on the actual picture. A pop-up menu will appear on the screen; then click on "view source." A new pop-up will appear that contains HTML computer code. At the bottom of all the HTML code, there is text that says "The following URL will result in display of this document." Right below that text will be a Web address starting with http://. It will always be located at the bottom of the page. Highlight the address and paste it into the address bar. Once the page is built, bookmark it and put it into computer favorites. By saving the page that way, it will be safely retrieved next time.

When creating a lesson plan that utilizes primary sources, keep it simple. At first, try to use only one primary source at a time. The lesson plans in this book are linked to national learning standards. On each lesson plan, a national learning standard has been correlated with the activity. When writing lesson plans, state standards can be linked to the lessons if desired.

Some items in the American Memory Collection on the Library of Congress Web site do have copyright restrictions. The library has included any information that pertains to ownership of the images. The library has also included any contact information necessary to gain permission to duplicate the item. Any questions regarding copyright issues with any of the materials on the Library of Congress Web site can be answered by contacting the Library of Congress through the e-mail contact form listed on its Web site.

There is one last thing to remember when using primary sources in the classroom. Every primary source used should teach students something. Don't print out primary sources just to use as classroom decorations. Primary sources are much more than decorations. They are learning tools from our past.

Differentiated Instruction

No teacher will argue that any two children are alike. Not only are all children different in looks and build, they are also different in how they learn. What works for one student does not always work for another. Students in the same classroom can have varying vocabulary knowledge. When differentiating instruction, various instructional vocabularies should be used. Too high a vocabulary can lose a student in discussion and activities. The children in a classroom have various reading levels. Taking these levels into consideration can improve the overall effectiveness of the lesson. Be aware of students' reading levels if asking them to read aloud. A student's self-esteem can severely drop if he or she is asked to read a passage higher than his or her reading level. Reading passages can be sent home to practice a few nights before they will be read aloud. This will give the student time to read and be familiar with the passage. For students with a relatively low reading level, the passage can be rewritten by the teacher at a lower reading level. In a differentiated classroom, various means of instruction are used, such as audio, text, and visuals. When creating a differentiated classroom, remember that the goal is to be flexible in teaching, planning, and evaluating students. Refer to the suggestions below:

Curriculum

- vary vocabulary usage and provide pictures as cues

Learning Activities and Extension Activities

Eastern Illinois University's Teaching with Primary Sources suggests various learning opportunities within the same concept. Suggestions include:

- Speeches
- Poems
- Mock newscasts
- Readers' theaters
- Plays
- Storytelling
- Debates
- Interviews
- Postcards
- Cartoons
- Logos or advertisements
- Maps
- T-shirt designs
- Murals
- Posters
- Dioramas
- 3-D models
- Collages
- Masks
- Inventions
- Multimedia presentations
- Commercials
- Documentaries
- Brochures
- Book covers
- Letters
- Alternate endings
- Newspaper articles
- Diary entries

CHAPTER 2

Lesson Plans Analyzing Primary Sources with Document Analysis Tools

All document analysis tools are located in the appendix.

Letter from Justin Butterfield to Abraham Lincoln

Written Document

Overview

An analysis of the written document will give students the chance to analyze a letter from Justin Butterfield to Abraham Lincoln. The students will use prior knowledge and decoding skills in order to comprehend the letter.

Objectives

After completing this lesson, the students will be able to:

- Consider the physical characteristics of the letter and what they tell about Justin Butterfield
- Gain understanding of the terminology
- Use an analysis tool

Time Required

One thirty-minute class period for discussion

Recommended Grade Level

Grades 4–8

Topics

Government, railroads, Abraham Lincoln

Era

National Expansion and Reform 1815–1860 time period

Standards

McREL 4th Edition Standards and Benchmarks

Historical Understanding

Understands and knows how to analyze chronological relationships and patterns

Understands the historical perspective

Understands how the Industrial Revolution, increasing immigration, the rapid expansion of slavery, and the westward movement changed American lives and led to regional tensions

Language Arts

Uses viewing and strategies to understand and interpret visual media

Uses grammatical and mechanical conventions in written compositions

Uses reading skills and strategies to understand and interpret a variety of literary texts

Working with Others

Displays effective interpersonal communication skills

Preparation

Have the following materials ready before the lesson:

- Prepare an overhead transparency of the primary source used or scan the image and display it through a projection unit
- Whiteboard, chalkboard, smart board, or chart tablet

Primary Source Used

To find this source, go to the American Memory home page and search for the title of this source: "Justin Butterfield to Abraham Lincoln, Sunday, February 27, 1848 (railroads)." The Abraham Lincoln Papers at the Library of Congress.

Primary Source Analysis Tool

Written document analysis and/or letter analysis

Procedure

(One class period)

1. When beginning the activity, involve the students in a discussion about railroads in the 1800s. Use the following questions as a basis for discussion:

    Why was it important to have railroads in the 1800s?

    How was grain and coal transported before railroads?

    In the 1840s, what steps would have to be taken to get a railroad in your area or state?

    Do you think some people were against the railroads? Why?

2. Introduce the primary source to the class. Give each student the primary source analysis tool (written document analysis). Explain to the students that they will be using the handout to analyze a written document from 1848. On the overhead projector or projection device, show a large version of the letter that Justin Butterfield wrote to Abraham Lincoln on Sunday, February 27, 1848. Then give each student his or her own copy of the written document along with a transcription of it.

3. Read the transcription of the document to the students as they follow along.
    Written documents give the students actual evidence of daily life in history. Go through the analysis tool with the class. Encourage the class to ask effective questions and discuss the possibilities of analysis. As the discussion expands, write responses and questions on the board. Encourage students to examine the letter. Some things to consider when doing this type of analysis:

    Ask the students to analyze the individual writing the letter.

    Did the author have good handwriting?

    Did the author cross out words? Why?

    What kind of personality traits can you get from the letter?

    What kind of terminology was used?

Extension

(One or two class periods)

- Have the students analyze the same letter using the letter analysis tool. Develop a hypothesis for discussion about why the railroads were an important part of the era.

- Give a three-minute persuasive speech to Lincoln about why your state needs a railroad.
- Work with other students and give a debate on the issue of railroads. Are they needed for the progression of the country? Or is it unnecessary for the country to continue growing? Who would benefit from the railroad? Would the railroads be a disservice to anyone?
- Make a poster about the benefits of the railroad.
- Create a multimedia presentation on Lincoln describing why your state needs a railroad.
- Write a letter to Lincoln giving your views of the railroad.

Evaluation

Assess the student extensions for evidence that they understood the importance of the railroad.

Assess the primary source analysis tool for evidence that they understood how to do the analysis.

Bill to Abolish Slavery

Written Document

Overview

An analysis of the written document will give students the chance to explain the bill that Abraham Lincoln wrote in order to abolish slavery in Washington, D.C. The students will use prior knowledge and decoding skills in order to comprehend the document.

Objectives

After completing this lesson, the students will be able to:

- Consider the physical characteristics of the document and what they can tell about Lincoln
- Gain understanding of the terminology
- Use an analysis tool

Time Required

One thirty-minute class period for discussion

Recommended Grade Level

Grades 4–8

Topics

Government, slavery, Abraham Lincoln

Era

National Expansion and Reform, 1815–1860 time period

Standards

McREL 4th Edition Standards and Benchmarks

Historical Understanding

Understands and knows how to analyze chronological relationships and patterns

Understands the historical perspective

Understands how the Industrial Revolution, increasing immigration, the rapid expansion of slavery, and the westward movement changed American lives and led to regional tensions

Language Arts

Uses viewing and strategies to understand and interpret visual media

Uses grammatical and mechanical conventions in written compositions

Uses reading skills and strategies to understand and interpret a variety of literary texts

Working with Others

Displays effective interpersonal communication skills

Preparation

Have the following materials ready before the lesson:

- Prepare an overhead transparency of the primary source used or scan the image and display it through a projection unit
- Whiteboard, chalkboard, smart board, or chart tablet to write student responses
- One copy of the primary source used for each student
- One copy of the translation of the primary source used for each student
- One copy of the analysis tool used for each student

Primary Source Used

To find this source, go to the American Memory home page and search for the title: "Abraham Lincoln [January 1849] (A Bill to Abolish Slavery in the District of Columbia)."

Primary Source Analysis Tool

Written document analysis and/or letter analysis

Procedure

(One class period)

1. When starting the activity, get students involved in the lesson by asking discussion questions:

    What president helped to abolish slavery?

    What areas of the United States were slave states?

    Why were slaves kept?

    What does abolish mean?

    Was this state a slave state?

2. Introduce the primary source to the class. Give each student the primary source analysis tool (written document analysis). Explain to the students that they will be using the handout to analyze a written document from Abraham Lincoln in 1849. On the overhead projector or projection device, show a large version of the bill that Abraham Lincoln wrote to abolish slavery in Washington, D.C. Then give each student his or her own copy of the written document along with a transcription of the document.

3. Read the transcription of the document to the students as they follow along.
   Go through the analysis tool with the class. Encourage them to ask effective questions and discuss the possibilities of analysis. As the discussion expands, write responses and questions on the board. As a class, write a hypothesis about the document. Encourage the students to examine the document in depth.

Extension

(One or two class periods)

- Use the letter analysis tool to analyze the document.
- Give a three-minute persuasive speech to Congress about why slavery should be abolished.
- Work with other students and give a debate on the issue of slavery. Present the debate to the class.
- Summarize the bill in your own words.
- Predict what happened next and draw conclusions about the situation.
- Create a PowerPoint presentation for Congress describing why slavery should be abolished.
- Draw an advertisement for abolishing slavery.

Evaluation

Assess the student extensions for evidence that they understood the importance of abolishing slavery.

Assess the primary source analysis tool(s) for evidence that the students understood how to do the analysis.

Speech Regarding the Mexican War

Written Document

Overview

An analysis of the written document will give students the chance to explain the speech Abraham Lincoln gave to Congress on January 12, 1848 regarding the Mexican War. The students will use prior knowledge and decoding skills in order to comprehend the document.

Objectives

After completing this lesson, the students will be able to:

- Consider the physical characteristics of the document and what they tell about the situation.
- Gain understanding of the terminology.
- Use an analysis tool.

Time Required

One thirty-minute class period for discussion

Recommended Grade Level

Grades 4–8

Topics

Government, Mexican War, Abraham Lincoln

Era

National Expansion and Reform, 1815–1860 time period

Standards

McREL 4th Edition Standards and Benchmarks

Historical Understanding

Understands and knows how to analyze chronological relationships and patterns

Understands the historical perspective

Understands how the Industrial Revolution, increasing immigration, the rapid expansion of slavery, and the westward movement changed American lives and led to regional tensions

Language Arts

Uses viewing and strategies to understand and interpret visual media

Uses grammatical and mechanical conventions in written compositions

Uses reading skills and strategies to understand and interpret a variety of literary texts

Working with Others

Displays effective interpersonal communication skills

Preparation

Have the following materials ready before the lesson:

- Prepare an overhead transparency of the primary source used or scan the image and display it through a projection unit
- Whiteboard, chalkboard, smart board, or chart tablet to write student responses
- One copy of the primary source used for each student
- One copy of the translation of the primary source used for each student
- One copy of the analysis tool used for each student

Primary Source Used

To find this source, go to the American Memory home page and search for the title: "Abraham Lincoln to Congress, January 12, 1848 (Speech regarding Mexican War)."

Primary Source Analysis Tool

Written document analysis

Procedure

(One class period)

1. Introduce the primary source to the class. Give each student the primary source analysis tool (written document analysis). Explain to the students that they will be using the handout to analyze a written document from Lincoln. On the overhead projector or projection device, show a large version of the speech that Lincoln gave regarding the Mexican War. Then give each student his or her own copy of the written document along with a transcription of the document.

2. Read the transcription of the document to the students as they follow along. Go through the analysis tool with the class. Encourage the students to ask effective questions and discuss the possibilities of analysis. As the discussion expands, write responses and questions on the board or tablet. As a class, write a hypothesis about the document. Encourage the students to really examine the document.

Extension

(One or two class periods)

- Write a review of the speech from the point of view of someone who actually heard it.
- Summarize the speech in your own words.
- Predict what happened next and draw conclusions about the situation.
- Write a newspaper article based on this written document.

Evaluation

Assess the student extensions for evidence that they understood the importance of this document.

Assess the primary source analysis tool(s) for evidence that the students understood how to do the analysis.

CHAPTER 3

Lesson Plans Using Rubrics to Evaluate Students' Performance

Letter to Elihu B. Washburne

Written Document

Overview

This activity will let the students participate in a related activity based on Abraham Lincoln's letter to Elihu B. Washburne, in which Lincoln discusses the recent loss of his Senate seat.

Objectives

After completing this lesson, the students will be able to:

Consider the physical characteristics of the letter and what they tell about Lincoln and the situation

Time Required

One or two thirty-minute class periods

Recommended Grade Level

Grades 4–8

Topics

Government, Abraham Lincoln

Era

National Expansion and Reform, 1815–1860 timeframe

Standards

McREL 4th Edition Standards and Benchmarks

Historical Understanding

Understands and knows how to analyze chronological relationships and patterns

Understands the historical perspective

Language Arts

Uses viewing and strategies to understand and interpret visual media

Uses grammatical and mechanical conventions in written compositions

Uses reading skills and strategies to understand and interpret a variety of literary texts

Working with Others

Displays effective interpersonal communication skills

Preparation

Have the following materials ready before the lesson:

- Prepare an overhead transparency of the primary source used or scan the image and display it through a projection unit
- Whiteboard, chalkboard, smart board, or chart tablet to write student responses
- One copy of the primary source used for each student
- One copy of the translation of the primary source used for each student

Primary Source Used

To find this primary source on the Library of Congress Web site, do a search on the American Memory home page. Search for Abraham Lincoln to Elihu B. Washburne, Friday, February 9, 1855 (Senate)—lost election.

Preactivity

A document analysis can be done on this primary source. Follow the format for document analysis in chapter 2—Document Analysis. Document analysis tools can be found in the appendix.

Activity

Give a mock newscast based on the letter and the loss of the Senate seat. This activity can be done after the preactivity or after this topic has been previously discussed from the textbook.

Procedure

(One class period)

1. Review the facts regarding Lincoln losing the Senate seat. Assign the following parts to the students:
   - Abraham Lincoln
   - Elihu B. Washburne
   - Field reporters
   - News anchors
   - Extras
   - Any additional role needed

2. What goes into a mock newscast? Have the students think of a real newscast from television. There are usually two anchors who give the latest news stories. For some stories, the anchors go to field reporters who are out in the actual area covering the news. News anchors have news stories typed up and on the desk in front of them. In a real newscast, a teleprompter shows the anchors the words as well. For this activity, the students should take on the various roles in order to put on a mock newscast. Research will have to be done on the subject (based on the primary source) in order to portray the accuracy of the newscast. When doing the newscast, the anchors will give a brief made-up story and then go to the field reporters for the interviews.

3. Have the students (field reporters) interview Abraham Lincoln and Washburne as if it is a real newscast. Students should write interview questions and be prepared to answer the questions. Students who are the reporters will have to take time to research and create appropriate questions. The students with the roles of Abraham Lincoln and Elihu B. Washburne will have to do research on the subject in order to answer the interview questions. The questions can be scripted so that the students playing Lincoln and Washburne will be prepared to answer the questions. Students should work together when scripting the interview questions. A setting can be created in the classroom or outside. Props and costumes can be used if desired.

4. The mock newscast should be arranged like a real television segment. The news anchors will finish a news story and go "live" to the field reporters who are with Lincoln and Washburne.

Extensions

(One or two class periods)

The students can choose to do the following:

- In two paragraphs, write a generalized statement of what the letter was about.
- Rewrite the letter in his or her own words.
- Predict what happened next and draw conclusions about the situation.
- Create a multimedia presentation on how to run for the U.S. Senate.
- Orally, evaluate the effectiveness of the letter as a persuasion. What are ways it was effective?

- Write a newspaper article that covers Lincoln losing the Senate seat.
- Describe what could have happened if Abraham Lincoln had become discouraged in politics after his loss and he didn't run for president.

Evaluation

Did the students understand how Abraham Lincoln losing the Senate seat was important and how it could have affected his political career or ambitions?

Use the rubric on page 19 to evaluate the mock newscast.

Rubric

	4	3	2	1
Facts	All facts are reported correctly (five of five).	Almost all facts are reported correctly (four of five).	Only two facts are reported correctly.	Lack of any facts.
Voice	Speaks clearly and correctly for the entire mock newscast.	Speaks clearly and correctly and pauses only briefly or mispronounces only two words.	Speaks clearly and correctly for about half of the newscast. Some words are mispronounced.	Does NOT speak clearly and correctly for almost the entire newscast and mispronounces many words.
Posture/Eye Contact	Stands or sits up straight while confident. Great eye contact with audience during almost all of the newscast/interview.	Stands or sits up straight. Good eye contact with audience during most of the newscast/interview.	Does not have good posture and appears too casual. Decent eye contact with audience during most of newscast/interview.	Does not have good posture and appears too casual. Little or no eye contact with audience during newscast/interview.
Emotion	Shows strong interest about the topic throughout the newscast.	Shows a strong interest about the topic throughout the newscast, but it seems overdone.	Shows some interest about the topic throughout the newscast.	Disinterest or boredom with the topic throughout the newscast.
Collaboration	All members of the group worked great. All members of the group almost always stayed on task.	All members of the group worked pretty well. All members of the group were almost always on task.	All members of the group worked well but the group was controlled by one or two group members. The group was almost always on task.	Group members off task. Group members were not involved in the group decisions.

From *Abraham Lincoln and His Era: Using the American Memory Project to Teach with Primary Sources* by Bobbi Ireland. Santa Barbara, CA: Libraries Unlimited. Copyright © 2010.

Letters Between Abraham Lincoln and Stephen Douglas

Written Document

Overview

Students will compare and contrast letters written back and forth between Abraham Lincoln and Stephen Douglas in 1858. The students will use prior knowledge and decoding skills in order to comprehend the documents.

Objectives

After completing this lesson, the students will be able to:

Compare and contrast the letters between Lincoln and Douglas

Gain understanding of the terminology

Time Required

One thirty-minute class period

Recommended Grade Level

Grades 4–8

Topics

Government, Abraham Lincoln

Era

National Expansion and Reform, 1815–1860 time period

Standards

McREL 4th Edition Standards and Benchmarks

Historical Understanding

Understands and knows how to analyze chronological relationships and patterns

Understands the historical perspective

Language Arts

Uses grammatical and mechanical conventions in written compositions

Uses reading skills and strategies to understand and interpret a variety of literary texts

Working with Others

Displays effective interpersonal communication skills

Preparation

Have the following materials ready before the lesson:

- Prepare an overhead transparency of the primary sources used or scan the images and display them through a projection unit
- Whiteboard, chalkboard, smart board, or chart tablet to write student responses
- One copy of each primary source used for each student
- One copy of the translation for each primary source used for each student

Primary Source Used

To find this primary source on the Library of Congress Web site, do a search on the American Memory home page. Search for Abraham Lincoln to Stephen A. Douglas, Saturday, July 24, 1858 (Debates), and reply from Stephen A. Douglas.

Preactivity

A document analysis can be done on this primary source. Follow the format for document analysis in chapter 2—Document Analysis. Document analysis tools can be found in the appendix.

Activity

Compare and contrast the letters. What was different about the two letters? Students should look at the letters' overall tone, grammar, and language. This activity should be done after the preactivity or after this topic has previously been discussed in the textbook.

Procedure

(One class period)

1. Lead the class in a discussion about the Lincoln and Douglas debates. Give each student a copy of the letters from Lincoln and Douglas. Read through the transcription of each.
2. Have the students work in pairs to compare and contrast the letters. The students will write an essay describing the similarities and differences. They will present the essay orally to the class. The students will turn in the written work in essay format.
3. Discuss "fact" and "opinion" with the class. The students will include facts and opinions in the essays.

Extensions

(One or two class periods)

The students can choose to do the following:

- Working together, one student will pretend to be Lincoln and one to be Douglas and orally re-create what is written in the letters.
- Predict what happened next after the letters were exchanged and draw conclusions about the situation. This is written in essay format.
- Evaluate the effectiveness of the letters. What was Lincoln's main point? Douglas? This is written in essay format.
- Write postcards in place of the letters.

Evaluation

Evaluate the compare and contrast essays with the rubric on page 23.

Rubric

	4	3	2	1
Categorizes Important Information	Lists all main points of the letters including several similarities and differences.	Lists all the main points of the letters including a few similarities and differences.	Lists one main point of the letters including one similarity and one difference.	Does not list any main points or similarities and differences.
Details	Includes several accurate details.	Includes a few accurate details.	Includes one accurate detail.	Does not include accurate details.
Facts	Lists four facts from the letters and has a clear understanding of why these are facts, and not opinions.	Lists three facts from the letters and has an understanding of why these are facts, and not opinions.	Lists two facts from the letters and does not seem to have an understanding of why these are facts, and not opinions.	Does not list facts from the letters.
Opinions	Lists four facts from the letters and has a clear understanding of why these are opinions, and not facts.	Lists three facts from the letters and has an understanding of why these are opinions, and not facts.	Lists two facts from the letters and does not seem to have an understanding of why these are opinions, and not facts.	Does not list facts from the letters.
Summarizing	Uses three to five complete sentences to summarize the letters.	Uses a few complete sentences to summarize the letters.	Able to summarize letters but seems to lack understanding.	Unable to summarize letters and lacks understanding of the activity.

From *Abraham Lincoln and His Era: Using the American Memory Project to Teach with Primary Sources* by Bobbi Ireland. Santa Barbara, CA: Libraries Unlimited. Copyright © 2010.

Letter from Joseph Medill

Written Document

Overview

The students will write a journal entry from Abraham Lincoln's point of view based on a letter written to Abraham Lincoln from Joseph Medill in 1858. The students will use prior knowledge and decoding skills in order to comprehend the letter.

Objectives

After completing this lesson, the students will be able to:

Gain an understanding of the letter

Gain understanding of the terminology

Time Required

One thirty-minute class period

Recommended Grade Level

Grades 4–8

Topics

Government, Abraham Lincoln, debates

Era

National Expansion and Reform, 1815–1860 time period

Standards

McREL 4th Edition Standards and Benchmarks

Historical Understanding

Understands and knows how to analyze chronological relationships and patterns

Understands the historical perspective

Language Arts

Uses viewing and strategies to understand and interpret visual media

Uses grammatical and mechanical conventions in written compositions

Uses reading skills and strategies to understand and interpret a variety of literary texts

Working with Others

Displays effective interpersonal communication skills

Preparation

Have the following materials ready before the lesson:

- Prepare an overhead transparency of the primary source used or scan the image and display it through a projection unit
- Whiteboard, chalkboard, smart board, or chart tablet to write student responses
- One copy of the primary source used for each student
- One copy of the translation of the primary source used for each student

Primary Source Used

To find this primary source on the Library of Congress Web site, do a search on the American Memory home page. Search for Joseph Medill and Abraham Lincoln (August 27, 1858) (Senate)—debate questions.

Preactivity

A document analysis can be done on this primary source. Follow the format for document analysis in chapter 2—Document Analysis. Document analysis tools can be found in the appendix.

Activity

The students will write a journal entry as Abraham Lincoln describing what he may have thought after reading the letter from Mr. Medill. This activity can be done after the preactivity or after this topic has been previously discussed from the textbook.

Procedure

(One class period)

1. Show the primary source on your projection device. Give each student a copy of the primary source. Read the transcription of the letter.
2. Lead the class in a discussion regarding the letter. The students will work independently and will write a journal from Abraham Lincoln's point of view.

Extension

(One or two class periods)

The students can choose to do the following:

- Predict what happened next and draw conclusions about the situation. This is written in essay format.
- Evaluate the effectiveness of the letter with oral discussion.
- Write a newspaper article in place of the letter.
- As Abraham Lincoln write a letter back to Joseph Medill stating his thoughts after reading the letter.

Evaluation

Did the students write a journal entry reacting to the letter? Follow the rubric on page 27 to evaluate the journal entry.

Rubric

	4	3	2	1
Sentences/ Paragraphs	Complete sentences, three to four well-written paragraphs.	Complete sentences without fragments or run-ons, two to three well-written paragraphs.	Mostly complete sentences with only a few sentence errors. Only two paragraphs.	Journal entry contained many sentence fragments or run-on sentences. Incomplete paragraphs or only one paragraph.
Introduction and Closing	Introduction and closing present.	Introduction and closing present.	Introduction and closing present.	Introduction and/ or closing are missing.
Grammar and Spelling	No errors in grammar or spelling.	Only one or two errors in grammar and/or spelling.	Three to four errors in grammar and/or spelling.	More than four errors in grammar and/or spelling.
Ideas	Clear and organized ideas. Journal entry easy to follow and understand.	Relatively clear and organized ideas. Journal entry easy to follow and understand.	Somewhat clear and organized ideas. Journal entry was not easy to follow and understand.	Unclear and disorganized ideas. Journal entry very hard to follow and understand.
Length	The journal entry is sixteen or more sentences.	The journal entry is ten to fifteen sentences.	The journal entry is five to ten sentences.	The journal entry is less than five sentences.
Capitalization/ Punctuation	No errors in capitalization/ punctuation.	One to two errors in capitalization/ punctuation.	Three to five errors in capitalization/ punctuation.	More than four errors in capitalization/ punctuation.
Neatness	Journal entry is very neatly written and very easy to read.	Journal entry is neatly written and easy to read.	Journal entry is readable but messy and maybe crinkled.	Journal entry is hard to read and the actual condition of the paper is a mess.
Content	Total understanding of the topic.	Good understanding of the topic.	Good understanding of only parts of the topic.	Lack of understanding of the topic.

From *Abraham Lincoln and His Era: Using the American Memory Project to Teach with Primary Sources* by Bobbi Ireland. Santa Barbara, CA: Libraries Unlimited. Copyright © 2010.

Popular Sovereignty

Written Document

Overview

This is a classroom activity based on Abraham Lincoln's speech on popular sovereignty that was written in 1858. This activity discusses values/rights of Americans. The students will use prior knowledge and decoding skills in order to comprehend the document.

Objectives

After completing this lesson, the students will be able to:

Understand the significance of the speech

Explore values/rights and discuss what they mean

Gain understanding of the terminology

Time Required

One thirty-minute class period

Recommended Grade Level

Grades 4–8

Topics

Government, Abraham Lincoln, speeches

Era

National Expansion and Reform, 1815–1860 time period

Standards

McREL 4th Edition Standards and Benchmarks

Historical Understanding

Understands and knows how to analyze chronological relationships and patterns

Understands the historical perspective

Understands how the Industrial Revolution, increasing immigration, the rapid expansion of slavery, and the westward movement changed American lives and led to regional tensions

Language Arts

Uses grammatical and mechanical conventions in written compositions

Uses reading skills and strategies to understand and interpret a variety of literary texts

Working with Others

Displays effective interpersonal communication skills

Preparation

Have the following materials ready before the lesson:

- Prepare an overhead transparency of the primary source used or scan the image and display it through a projection unit
- Whiteboard, chalkboard, smart board, or chart tablet to write student responses
- One copy of the primary source used for each student
- One copy of the translation of the primary source used for each student

Primary Source Used

To find this primary source on the Library of Congress Web site, do a search on the American Memory home page. Search for Abraham Lincoln, May 18, 1858 (draft of speech on popular sovereignty).

Preactivity

A document analysis can be done on this primary source. Follow the format for document analysis in chapter 2—Document Analysis. Document analysis tools can be found in the appendix.

Activity

The students will discuss and explore American values and rights. This activity can be done after the preactivity or after this topic has been previously discussed from the textbook.

Procedure

(One class period)

1. Show the primary source to the class. Read the transcription as the students follow along. Give each student a copy of the primary source. Lead the class in a discussion about what it means to be an American. Encourage discussion about American values and rights.

2. The students will make a chart on a piece of paper listing important American values and rights. Have the students write "Values and Rights" on the top of the paper. Next, make a list of specific rights and values and what the students do to exercise those values/rights. If the students do not exercise a particular value/right, they will write down what they "could" do in order to exercise it. This can be done independently or during the group discussion.

3. After the chart is completed, the students will choose the value/right that is most important to them and write an essay describing it and why it is important to them. The students will present it orally to the class.

Extension

(One or two class periods)

The students can choose to do the following:

- Write a newspaper article posing as a reporter who talked to Abraham Lincoln regarding the speech
- Write a journal entry as Abraham Lincoln describing what you think he thought after writing the speech

Evaluation

Was the chart completed?

Was a clear, well-planned essay written? Use the rubric on page 31. This rubric evaluates the process as well as the final product. Be sure to observe and monitor the students during both the planning and working stages.

Rubric

	4	3	2	1
Emotion	Shows a strong interest about the topic throughout the presentation.	Shows a strong interest about the topic throughout the presentation, but it seems overdone.	Shows some interest about the topic throughout the presentation.	Disinterest or boredom with the topic throughout the presentation.
Voice	Speaks clearly and correctly for the entire presentation.	Speaks clearly and correctly and pauses only briefly or mispronounces only two words.	Speaks clearly and correctly for about half of the presentation. Some words are mispronounced.	Does NOT speak clearly and correctly for almost the entire presentation and mispronounces many words.
Vocabulary	Appropriate and varied vocabulary used.	Appropriate and somewhat varied vocabulary used.	Appropriate vocabulary but did not vary word usage.	Weak vocabulary and used same words throughout the presentation.
Topic	On topic all of the time.	On topic most of the time.	On topic some of the time.	Unrecognizable topic.
Volume	Loud enough to be heard by all throughout the presentation.	Loud enough to be heard by all audience members most of the time.	Loud enough to be heard by all audience members some of the time.	Could not be heard because of low volume level.
Posture/Eye Contact	Stands up straight, looks relaxed yet confident. Great eye contact during the presentation.	Stands up straight, somewhat confident. Good eye contact with during the presentation.	Stands up straight occasionally. Some eye contact during the presentation.	Slouches. No eye contact during the presentation.
Planning	Completely prepared. Practiced for presentation.	Well prepared for presentation.	Fairly prepared for the presentation.	Not prepared for the presentation.
Content	Total understanding of topic.	Good understanding of topic.	Good understanding of only parts of the topic.	Lack of understanding of the topic.

From *Abraham Lincoln and His Era: Using the American Memory Project to Teach with Primary Sources* by Bobbi Ireland. Santa Barbara, CA: Libraries Unlimited. Copyright © 2010.

Congratulation Letters

Written Document

Overview

The students will use congratulation letters to plan a congratulation party for Abraham Lincoln. The students will use prior knowledge and decoding skills in order to comprehend the letters.

Objectives

After completing this lesson, the students will be able to:

Read and comprehend the congratulation letters

Research the era and find era specific snacks and decoration ideas

Gain understanding of the terminology

Time Required

Two to three thirty-minute class periods for planning and implementation

Recommended Grade Level

Grades 4–8

Topics

Government, Abraham Lincoln

Era

National Expansion and Reform, 1815–1860 time period

Standards

McREL 4th Edition Standards and Benchmarks

Historical Understanding

Understands the historical perspective

Understands how the Industrial Revolution, increasing immigration, the rapid expansion of slavery, and the westward movement changed American lives and led to regional tensions

Language Arts

Uses viewing and strategies to understand and interpret visual media

Uses grammatical and mechanical conventions in written compositions

Uses reading skills and strategies to understand and interpret a variety of literary texts

Working with Others

Displays effective interpersonal communication skills

Preparation

Have the following materials ready before the lesson:

- Prepare an overhead transparency of the primary sources used or scan the images and display them through a projection unit
- Whiteboard, chalkboard, smart board, or chart tablet to write student responses
- One copy of each primary source used for each student
- One copy of each translation of the primary sources used for each student

Primary Sources Used

To find these primary sources on the Library of Congress Web site, do a search on the American Memory home page. Search for John B. Fry to Abraham Lincoln, Thursday, August 9, 1860 (congratulations from an old friend), Joshua F. Speed to Abraham Lincoln, Wednesday, November 14, 1860 (congratulations), Thurlow Weed to Abraham Lincoln, Wednesday, November 7, 1860 (election results and political advice), and James W. Jones to Abraham Lincoln, Tuesday, December 11, 1860 (congratulations and cabinet advice from Virginia).

Preactivity

A document analysis can be done on this primary source. Follow the format for document analysis in chapter 2—Document Analysis. Document analysis tools can be found in the appendix.

Activity

The students will discuss and explore the 1860 era. This activity can be done after the preactivity or after this topic has been previously discussed from the textbook.

Procedure

(One class period)

1. Show the students the primary sources to the class. Give copies of the primary sources to the students. Read the transcription of the sources. Briefly discuss the tone of the letters.

2. Ask the students how we celebrate good news. Discuss celebrations and how they differ in other countries, regions, and even in families. Discuss how a celebration might have been held for Abraham Lincoln in 1860. The student will write a short congratulation letter to Mr. Lincoln.

3. Split up the class into working groups. Each group will be responsible for researching celebrations in the 1860s, for example, attire, food, decorations, and music. Each group will find ideas to use in a recreated classroom celebration for Mr. Lincoln.

4. After group research is finished and ideas are made, the groups will work together to plan and organize a celebration with 1860 era inspired food, music, and decorations.

5. Have an 1860 inspired classroom celebration party for Abraham Lincoln. During the celebration, the students will read their congratulation letters.

Extension

(One or two class periods)

The students can choose to do the following:

- Evaluate the effectiveness of the letters by giving an oral report. What letter did the student like best and why?

- Write a journal entry as Abraham Lincoln describing what he thought after winning and then after receiving congratulation letters.

Evaluation

Were the students able to find 1860 resources?

Did the students work in groups to create a 1860 inspired celebration? Use the rubric on page 35. The rubric evaluates the process as well as the final product. Be sure to observe and monitor students during the planning stages and actual work time.

Students will write a self reflection of the planning and work process.

Groups will write a group reflection of the planning and work process. How did the group work together? Did one person do all the work? Did the group mesh well together?

Rubric

	4	3	2	1
Collaboration	Provided useful ideas and participated in group discussion.	Usually provided useful ideas and participated in group discussion.	Sometimes provided useful ideas and participated somewhat in group discussion.	Did not provide much useful ideas or participate in group discussion.
Time Management	Manages time well. Is a positive addition to the group in meeting deadlines and responsibilities.	Somewhat manages time well. Was a small help and addition to the group in meeting deadlines and responsibilities.	Does not manage time well and has to be urged to keep working.	Does not manage time well even with reminders to keep working. Keeps the group from meeting deadlines and responsibilities.
Attitude	Very positive attitude regarding the project.	Often has a positive attitude of the project.	Usually has a positive attitude of the project but has been negative a few times.	Often negative regarding the project.
Focus	Self-starter, leader, and very focused on the task at hand.	Very focused on the task at hand. Does what is asked to do.	Somewhat focused on the task. Reminders needed to stay focused.	Lack of focus. Lets others do the work.
Preparedness	Always brings the needed classroom materials to class that are needed.	Almost always brings the needed classroom materials to class that are needed.	Usually brings the needed classroom materials to class but needs to be told to get to work.	Does not bring needed classroom materials to class. Even when told to get to work, seldom gets busy.
Working with Others	Almost always listens, shares, and contributes with the group. A great addition in the group.	Usually listens, shares, and contributes with the group. A good addition in the group.	Sometimes listens, shares, and contributes with the group.	Rarely listens, shares, and contributes with the group.
Content	Total understanding of topic.	Good understanding of topic.	Good understanding of only parts of the topic.	Lack of understanding of the topic.

From *Abraham Lincoln and His Era: Using the American Memory Project to Teach with Primary Sources* by Bobbi Ireland. Santa Barbara, CA: Libraries Unlimited. Copyright © 2010.

Letter from Julia Matie

Written Document

Overview

The students will use the primary source as a base to create a multimedia presentation. The primary source is a letter written by Julia Matie discussing how she opposed Abraham's inauguration. The students will also analyze an addendum that was written in addition to the letter by B. Todd in 1863. The students will use prior knowledge and decoding skills in order to comprehend the document.

Objectives

After completing this lesson, the students will be able to:

Consider the physical characteristics of the letter and gain an understanding of what is being said

Create a multimedia presentation showing why people were against and for the election of Abraham Lincoln

Gain understanding of the terminology

Time Required

One or two thirty-minute class periods for discussion

Recommended Grade Level

Grades 4–8

Topics

Government, Abraham Lincoln

Era

Civil War and reconstruction, 1861–1877 time period

Standards

McREL 4th Edition Standards and Benchmarks

Historical Understanding

Understands and knows how to analyze chronological relationships and patterns

Understands the historical perspective

Understands how the Industrial Revolution, increasing immigration, the rapid expansion of slavery, and the westward movement changed American lives and led to regional tensions

Language Arts

Uses viewing and strategies to understand and interpret visual media

Uses grammatical and mechanical conventions in written compositions

Uses reading skills and strategies to understand and interpret a variety of literary texts

Working with Others

Displays effective interpersonal communication skills

Preparation

Have the following materials ready before the lesson:

- Prepare an overhead transparency of the primary source used or scan the image and display it through a projection unit
- Whiteboard, chalkboard, smart board, or chart tablet to write student responses
- One copy of each primary source used for each student
- One copy of each translation of the primary source used for each student

Primary Source Used

To find this primary source on the Library of Congress Web site, do a search on the American Memory home page. Search for Julia Matie to Mrs. A. M. Thomas, Tuesday, January 8, 1861 (opposes Lincoln's inauguration. Addendum written by B. Todd, May 13, 1863).

Preactivity

A document analysis can be done on this primary source. Follow the format for document analysis in chapter 2—Document Analysis. Document analysis tools can be found in the appendix.

Activity

The students will discuss and review the primary source. Lead the class in a discussion about people being for and against the election of Abraham Lincoln. The students will work in learning groups to create a multimedia presentation showing why people had varying opinions of the president. This activity can be done after the preactivity or after this topic has been previously discussed from the textbook.

Procedure

(One class period)

1. Show the primary source to the students on the projection device. Review important points of the primary source. Ask the students why people were for and against Abraham Lincoln. Write their responses down.

2. Split the class into learning groups. Each group will create a multimedia presentation showing the events that lead up to the inauguration of Abraham Lincoln. The students should include points used in the primary source by Ms. Matie as to why she was against it. The students will include several reasons why people were for and against Mr. Lincoln. Additional research can be done as a group or as individuals.

3. After the learning groups have created the presentations, each group will show the presentations to the class.

Extension

(One or two class periods)

The students can choose to do the following:

- Find an additional primary source on the Library of Congress Web site that expresses support or concern for Lincoln's inauguration.

- Write an essay describing the student's feelings on Abraham Lincoln becoming president. Is the student for or against Mr. Lincoln? Why?

Evaluation

Was a group multimedia presentation successfully completed? Refer to the rubric on page 39.

Rubric

	4	3	2	1
Background	Choice of background colors is excellent and eye-catching but not distracting.	Choice of background colors is good and eye-catching but not distracting.	Choice of background colors is eye-catching but somewhat distracting.	Choice of background colors is overwhelming and distracting.
Sounds	Great sounds are used. They add much to the overall feel of the presentation. Great volume level.	Great sounds are used. They add much to the overall feel of the presentation. Volume level could be adjusted (higher or lower).	Good sounds are used. More or less sounds could have been used. Volume level could be adjusted (higher or lower).	Sounds were not utilized appropriately in the presentation. Volume level needed adjusted (higher or lower).
Quality	Very good quality presentation. Unique and original.	Good quality presentation. Unique and original.	Good quality presentation. Could have been more unique and original.	Better quality of work needed. Lacked originality and uniqueness.
Text/Font	Font formats chosen wisely. Font, color, and size all worked to contribute to the overall presentation. Very easily read.	Font formats chosen well. Font, color, and size all worked to contribute to the overall presentation. Very easily read.	Font formats chosen could have been less. Font, color, and size seemed a little too much for the overall presentation. A little hard to read.	Too many font formats. Font, color, and size was too much for the overall presentation. Very hard to read.
Content	Accurate information presented in the presentation. No factual errors.	Mostly accurate information presented in the presentation. No factual errors.	Mostly accurate information presented in the presentation. A few factual errors.	Mostly accurate information presented in the presentation. Several factual errors.
Sequencing	All information is in logical sequence. Very easy to follow.	Most information is in logical sequence. Easy to follow.	Information is not all in logical sequence. Not always easy to follow.	Information is not in logical sequence. Not easy to follow.
Effect	The presentation is very effective. A good understanding of the topic was achieved by the audience.	The presentation is effective. A good understanding of the topic was achieved by the audience.	The presentation is fairly effective. An understanding of the topic was not achieved by the audience.	The presentation is not effective. More parts could have been added. An understanding of the topic was not achieved by the audience.

From *Abraham Lincoln and His Era: Using the American Memory Project to Teach with Primary Sources* by Bobbi Ireland. Santa Barbara, CA: Libraries Unlimited. Copyright © 2010.

Letter Written by Grace Bedell

Written Document

Overview

The students will create a comic strip based on a letter written by Grace Bedell. She was a little girl who wrote Abraham Lincoln a letter telling him that he should grow a beard or whiskers, as she called it. When making the comic strip, the students will also use information from a letter that Lincoln wrote back to Grace. The letters were written in 1860. The students will use prior knowledge and decoding skills in order to comprehend the document.

Objectives

After completing this lesson, the students will be able to:

Understand the significance of the letter written to Lincoln

Gain understanding of the terminology

Use the information in primary source to create a comic strip

Time Required

One or two thirty-minute class periods for discussion

Recommended Grade Level

Grades 4–8

Topics

Government, Abraham Lincoln

Era

National Expansion and Reform, 1815–1860 time period

Standards

McREL 4th Edition Standards and Benchmarks

Historical Understanding

Understands and knows how to analyze chronological relationships and patterns

Understands the historical perspective

Language Arts

Uses viewing and strategies to understand and interpret visual media

Uses grammatical and mechanical conventions in written compositions

Uses reading skills and strategies to understand and interpret a variety of literary texts

Working with Others

Displays effective interpersonal communication skills

Preparation

Have the following materials ready before the lesson:

- Prepare an overhead transparency of the primary sources used or scan the image and display them through a projection unit
- Whiteboard, chalkboard, smart board, or chart tablet to write student responses
- One copy of each primary source used for each student
- One copy of each translation of the primary sources used for each student

Primary Sources Used

To find these primary sources on the Library of Congress Web site, do a search on the American Memory home page. Search for Grace Bedell to Abraham Lincoln, Thursday, October 18, 1860 (typed copy) and Abraham Lincoln to Grace Bedell, Friday, October 19, 1860 (reply to Bedell's letter concerning Lincoln's beard).

Preactivity

A document analysis can be done on this primary source. Follow the format for document analysis in chapter 2—Document Analysis. Document analysis tools can be found in the appendix.

Activity

The students will discuss and review the primary source. They will interpret the information in the primary source to use creative expression skills in creating a comic strip. This activity can be done after the preactivity or after this topic has been previously discussed from the textbook.

Procedure

(One class period)

1. Display the primary source on the projector. Briefly review the letters with the class. Discuss how the letter could have been a critical turning point in Lincoln's appearance. Ask the students what they would do if someone asked them to change their appearance. Would they be mad, annoyed, or would it be funny?

2. The students will create a comic strip based on this primary source. Encourage the students to be creative with dialogue. The students are not graded on artistic ability, but rather on understanding the information in the primary source and recreating it in the comic strip.

Extension

(One or two class periods)

The students can choose to do the following:

- Predict what happened next and draw conclusions about the situation.
- Evaluate the effectiveness of the letters. What was their purpose?
- Write an essay answering the question: Would Abraham Lincoln have been viewed differently if he didn't have a beard?
- Give an oral presentation answering the question: Do you believe Grace was the reason he grew a beard?

Evaluation

Use the rubric on page 43 to evaluate the comic strip.

Rubric

	4	3	2	1
Overall Project	Makes a complete comic strip describing the subject matter in the primary source.	Makes a complete comic strip of most of the subject matter in the primary source.	Makes a complete comic strip describing some of the subject matter in the primary source.	Comic strip is not complete and does not describe the subject matter in the primary source.
Interpretation	Able to interpret the primary source and recreate it in a comic strip form.	Able to interpret most of the primary source and recreate it in a comic strip form.	Able to interpret some of the primary source and recreate it in a comic strip form.	Was not able to interpret the primary source and recreate it in a comic strip form.
Neatness	Impressive expression, creativity, design, and communication of ideas.	Good expression, creativity, design, and communication of ideas.	Fair expression, creativity, design, and communication of ideas.	Lack of expression, creativity, design, and communication of ideas.
Content	Accurate information is presented. No factual errors.	Mostly accurate information is presented. No factual errors.	Mostly accurate information is presented. A few factual errors.	Mostly accurate information is presented. Several factual errors.

From *Abraham Lincoln and His Era: Using the American Memory Project to Teach with Primary Sources* by Bobbi Ireland. Santa Barbara, CA: Libraries Unlimited. Copyright © 2010.

Abraham Lincoln's First Inaugural Address

Written Document

Overview

The students will use the first and final drafts of Abraham Lincoln's first inaugural address to create a T-shirt in support of Lincoln's election as president. The documents were written in 1861. The students will use prior knowledge and decoding skills in order to comprehend the documents.

Objectives

After completing this lesson, the students will be able to:

Observe each document and find similarities and differences between the two

Find powerful words that were used in the documents

Summarize what they have learned

Gain understanding of the terminology

Use an analysis tool

Time Required

One or two thirty-minute class periods for discussion

Recommended Grade Level

Grades 4–8

Topics

Government, Abraham Lincoln

Era

Civil War and Reconstruction, 1861–1877 time period

Standards

McREL 4th Edition Standards and Benchmarks

Historical Understanding

Understands and knows how to analyze chronological relationships and patterns

Understands the historical perspective

Understands how the industrial revolution, increasing immigration, the rapid expansion of slavery, and the westward movement changed American lives and led to regional tensions

Language Arts

Uses viewing and strategies to understand and interpret visual media

Uses grammatical and mechanical conventions in written compositions

Uses reading skills and strategies to understand and interpret a variety of literary texts

Working with Others

Displays effective interpersonal communication skills

Preparation

Have the following materials ready before the lesson:

- Prepare an overhead transparency of the primary sources used or scan the images and display them through a projection unit
- Whiteboard, chalkboard, smart board, or chart tablet to write student responses
- One copy of each primary source used for each student
- One copy of each translation of the primary sources used for each student
- One copy of the analysis tool used for each student
- One white T-shirt for each student
- Fabric paints in various colors
- Paintbrushes

Primary Sources Used

To find this primary source on the Library of Congress Web site, do a search on the American Memory home page. Search for Abraham Lincoln, January–February 1861 (first inaugural address, first printed draft) and Abraham Lincoln [March 1861] (first inaugural address, final version).

Preactivity

A document analysis can be done on this primary source. Follow the format for document analysis in chapter 2—Document Analysis. Document analysis tools can be found in the appendix.

Activity

The students will discuss and review the primary source. Lead the class in a discussion regarding Lincoln's inauguration. The students will use the first and final drafts of Lincoln's first inaugural address to create a T-shirt in support of Lincoln's election as president. This activity can be done after the preactivity or after this topic has been previously discussed from the textbook.

Procedure

(One class period)

1. Show the primary source to the class on the projection device. Read the transcription of the primary source while the students follow along. Lead the class in a discussion about presidential elections. Talk about the ways elections have changed since Lincoln ran for president and was inaugurated. During the discussion, have students find powerful words used in the documents.

2. Following the discussion, explain to the students they are going to plan, design, and paint a T-shirt in support for Abraham Lincoln. It can be a shirt promoting his election or celebrating his inauguration. Students should use powerful words to promote his election or in celebration.

Extension

(One or two class periods)

The students can choose to do the following:

- Write newspaper articles as a reporter who heard the final speech.
- Predict what happened next and draw conclusions about the situation.
- Evaluate the effectiveness of the speech. What was the purpose of the speech?
- Create a multimedia presentation that explains the main points of the speech.

Evaluation

Assess the student extensions for evidence that they understood what was expected.

Refer to the rubric on page 47 when evaluating the T-shirt design. The rubric includes process and product evaluations. Be sure to observe and monitor students during the planning and designing stages of the project.

Rubric

	4	3	2	1
Planning/ Organization	Took adequate time in planning and organizing the design for the T-shirt.	Took some time in planning and organizing the design for the T-shirt, but had to be reminded to continue working.	Took a fair amount of time in planning and organizing the design for the T-shirt. Needed several reminders to continue working.	Went right into painting on the T-shirt without any preplanning or organization.
Thematic Accuracy	The student's design fits into the theme of the assignment perfectly.	The student's design fits into the theme of the assignment well.	Portions of the student's design fit into the theme of the assignment.	The student's design does not fit into the theme of the assignment.
Color	The colors in the T-shirt work well together.	The colors in the T-shirt work good together.	The colors in the T-shirt work good together but more/ less colors could have been used.	The colors in the T-shirt do not coordinate together or work for the overall presentation.
Time/Effort	Used time wisely. The student took the assignment seriously.	Used time wisely. The student took the assignment fairly seriously.	Did not always use time wisely. The student did not always take the assignment seriously.	Time not used wisely. The student did not take the assignment seriously.

From *Abraham Lincoln and His Era: Using the American Memory Project to Teach with Primary Sources* by Bobbi Ireland. Santa Barbara, CA: Libraries Unlimited. Copyright © 2010.

Letter by Mrs. Luther Fowler

Written Document

Overview

The students will use a letter written to Abraham Lincoln from Mrs. Luther Fowler, a former slave as inspiration to write a letter to Abraham Lincoln as a former slave owner. The document was written in 1865. The students will use prior knowledge and decoding skills in order to comprehend the document.

Objectives

After completing this lesson, the students will be able to:

Summarize what they have learned

Gain understanding of the terminology

Write a letter

Time Required

One or two thirty-minute class periods for discussion

Recommended Grade Level

Grades 4–8

Topics

Government, Abraham Lincoln

Era

Civil War and Reconstruction, 1861–1877 time period

Standards

McREL 4th Edition Standards and Benchmarks

Historical Understanding

Understands and knows how to analyze chronological relationships and patterns

Understands the historical perspective

Understands how the Industrial Revolution, increasing immigration, the rapid expansion of slavery, and the westward movement changed American lives and led to regional tensions

Language Arts

Uses viewing and strategies to understand and interpret visual media

Uses grammatical and mechanical conventions in written compositions

Uses reading skills and strategies to understand and interpret a variety of literary texts

Working with Others

Displays effective interpersonal communication skills

Preparation

Have the following materials ready before the lesson:

- Prepare an overhead transparency of the primary source used or scan the image and display it through a projection unit
- Whiteboard, chalkboard, smart board, or chart tablet to write student responses
- One copy of each primary source used for each student
- One copy of each translation of the primary source used for each student

Primary Source Used

To find this primary source on the Library of Congress Web site, do a search on the American Memory home page. Search for Mrs. Luther Fowler [George Washington] to Abraham Lincoln, Sunday, March 19, 1865 (writes on behalf of freed men at Hilton Head).

Preactivity

A document analysis can be done on this primary source. Follow the format for document analysis in chapter 2—Document Analysis. Document analysis tools can be found in the appendix.

Activity

The students will discuss and review the primary source. The students will write a letter with the point of view of a former slave owner. This activity can be done after the preactivity or after this topic has been previously discussed from the textbook.

Procedure

(One class period)

1. Show the primary source to the students. Read the transcription aloud. Lead the class in a discussion about the freedom of slaves and slaveowners. Refer to the primary source for a basis on how the slaves felt after freedom. Discuss how the slave owners may have felt. Were some slave owners mad? Sad? We hear how many slave owners were abusive, but were they all that way?

2. The students will write a letter from a former slave owner to Lincoln. The students can take the point of view of a former slave owner who treated the slaves well, and is sad to see them go. Or they can take the point of view of a former slave owner who is angry that his or her slaves are free.

Extension

(One or two class periods)

The students can choose to do the following:

- Make a poster celebrating the freedom of the slaves.
- Predict what happened next and draw conclusions about the situation.
- Evaluate the effectiveness of the letter. What was the purpose?
- Make a painting showing the freedom of slaves.
- Write a letter to Lincoln from the point of view of a former slave.

Evaluation

Refer to the rubric on page 51 to evaluate the letter:

Rubric

	4	3	2	1
Sentences/ Paragraphs	Complete sentences. Three to four well-written paragraphs.	Complete sentences without fragments or run-ons. Two to three well-written paragraphs.	Mostly complete sentences with only a few sentence errors. Only two paragraphs.	Letter contained many sentence fragments or run-on sentences. Incomplete paragraphs or only one paragraph.
Introduction and Closing	Introduction and closing present.	Introduction and closing present.	Introduction and closing present.	Introduction and/or closing are missing.
Grammar and Spelling	No errors in grammar or spelling.	Only one or two errors in grammar and/or spelling.	Three to four errors in grammar and/or spelling.	More than four errors in grammar and/or spelling.
Ideas	Clear and organized ideas. Letter easy to follow and understand.	Relatively clear and organized ideas. Letter easy to follow and understand.	Somewhat clear and organized ideas. Letter was not easy to follow and understand.	Unclear and disorganized ideas. Letter very hard to follow and understand.
Capitalization/ Punctuation	No errors in capitalization/ punctuation.	One to two errors in capitalization/ punctuation.	Three to four errors in capitalization/ punctuation.	More than four errors in capitalization/ punctuation.
Neatness	Letter is very neat and easily readable.	Letter is neat and easily readable.	Letter is fairly easy to read.	Letter is not easy to read and is in poor condition.
Content	Accurate information presented. No factual errors.	Mostly accurate information presented. No factual errors.	Mostly accurate information presented. A few factual errors.	Mostly accurate information presented. Several factual errors.

From *Abraham Lincoln and His Era: Using the American Memory Project to Teach with Primary Sources* by Bobbi Ireland. Santa Barbara, CA: Libraries Unlimited. Copyright © 2010.

Emancipation Proclamation

Written Document

Overview

The students will explain and discuss Abraham Lincoln's Emancipation Proclamation. The document was written in 1863. After discussion, the class will write a newspaper article summarizing the main points of the primary source. The students will use prior knowledge and decoding skills in order to comprehend the document.

Objectives

After completing this lesson, the students will be able to:

Find powerful words that were used in the document

Summarize what they have learned

Gain understanding of the terminology

Time Required

One or two thirty-minute class periods for discussion

Recommended Grade Level

Grades 4–8

Topics

Government, Abraham Lincoln

Era

Civil War and Reconstruction, 1861–1877 time period

Standards

McREL 4th Edition Standards and Benchmarks

Historical Understanding

Understands and knows how to analyze chronological relationships and patterns

Understands the historical perspective

Understands how the Industrial Revolution, increasing immigration, the rapid expansion of slavery, and the westward movement changed American lives and led to regional tensions

Language Arts

Uses viewing and strategies to understand and interpret visual media

Uses grammatical and mechanical conventions in written compositions

Uses reading skills and strategies to understand and interpret a variety of literary texts

Working with Others

Displays effective interpersonal communication skills

Preparation

Have the following materials ready before the lesson:

- Prepare an overhead transparency of the primary source used or scan the image and display it through a projection unit
- Whiteboard, chalkboard, smart board, or chart tablet to write student responses
- One copy of each primary source used for each student
- One copy of each translation of the primary source used for each student

Primary Sources Used

To find this primary source on the Library of Congress Web site, do a search on the American Memory home page. Search for Abraham Lincoln, Thursday, January 1, 1863 (final Emancipation Proclamation—final draft [lithograph copy].

Preactivity

A document analysis can be done on this primary source. Follow the format for document analysis in chapter 2—Document Analysis. Document analysis tools can be found in the appendix.

Activity

The students will discuss and review the primary source. Lead the class in a discussion about the Emancipation Proclamation. Afterward, the students will write a newspaper article summarizing the main points of the primary source. This activity can be done after the preactivity or after this topic has been previously discussed from the textbook.

Procedure

(One class period)

1. Show the class the primary source on the projection device. Read over the transcription while the students follow along. Lead the class in a discussion about the Emancipation Proclamation. Help the students find the main points of the document.

2. After discussion, the students will write a newspaper article summarizing the primary source. Pick a name for your newspaper. When finished, compile all of the newspaper articles for a display in the hallway or classroom.

Extension

(One or two class periods)

The students can choose to do the following:

• Predict what happened next and draw conclusions about the situation.

• Evaluate the effectiveness of the speech. What was the purpose of the speech?

• Create a multimedia presentation that explains the main points of the speech.

Evaluation

Assess the student extensions for evidence that they understood what was expected.

Refer to the rubric on page 55 when evaluating the newspaper article.

Rubric

	4	3	2	1
Sentences/ Paragraphs	Complete sentences. Three to four well-written paragraphs.	Complete sentences without fragments or run-ons. Two to three well-written paragraphs.	Mostly complete sentences with only a few sentence errors. Only two paragraphs.	Article contained many sentence fragments or run-on sentences. Incomplete paragraphs or only one paragraph.
Introduction and Closing	Introduction and closing are present.	Introduction and closing are present.	Introduction and closing are present.	Introduction and/or closing are missing.
Grammar and Spelling	No errors in grammar or spelling.	Only one to two errors in grammar and/or spelling.	Three to four errors in grammar and/or spelling.	More than four errors in grammar and/or spelling.
Ideas	Clear and organized ideas. Article easy to follow and understand.	Relatively clear and organized ideas. Article easy to follow and understand.	Somewhat clear and organized ideas. Article was not easy to follow and understand.	Unclear and disorganized ideas. Article very hard to follow and understand.
Length	The article is more than seven paragraphs long.	The article is five to six paragraphs long.	The article is three to four paragraphs long.	The article is one to two paragraphs long.
Capitalization/ Punctuation	No errors in capitalization/ punctuation.	One to two errors in capitalization/ punctuation.	Three to four errors in capitalization/ punctuation.	More than four errors in capitalization/ punctuation.
Neatness	Article is typed and neat.	Article is neatly handwritten.	Article is typed but messy and maybe crinkled.	Article is typed but the actual condition of the paper is a mess.
Content	Accurate information presented. No factual errors.	Mostly accurate information presented. No factual errors.	Mostly accurate information presented. A few factual errors.	Mostly accurate information presented. Several factual errors.

From *Abraham Lincoln and His Era: Using the American Memory Project to Teach with Primary Sources* by Bobbi Ireland. Santa Barbara, CA: Libraries Unlimited. Copyright © 2010.

Letter from Ulysses S. Grant about the First African American Troops

Written Document

Overview

The students will write a letter to Abraham Lincoln from the point of view of a former slave who wants to enlist in the military. This letter is based on the information regarding Abraham Lincoln's decision to enlist the first black troops in the South. The primary source was written in 1863 by Ulysses S. Grant as a letter to Abraham Lincoln. The students will use prior knowledge and decoding skills in order to comprehend the document.

Objectives

After completing this lesson, the students will be able to:

Summarize what they have learned

Gain understanding of the terminology

Time Required

One or two thirty-minute class periods for discussion

Recommended Grade Level

Grades 4–8

Topics

Government, Abraham Lincoln

Era

Civil War and Reconstruction, 1861–1877 time period

Standards

McREL 4th Edition Standards and Benchmarks

Historical Understanding

Understands and knows how to analyze chronological relationships and patterns

Understands the historical perspective

Understands how the Industrial Revolution, increasing immigration, the rapid expansion of slavery, and the westward movement changed American lives and led to regional tensions

Language Arts

Uses viewing and strategies to understand and interpret visual media

Uses grammatical and mechanical conventions in written compositions

Uses reading skills and strategies to understand and interpret a variety of literary texts

Working with Others

Displays effective interpersonal communication skills

Preparation

Have the following materials ready before the lesson:

- Prepare an overhead transparency of the primary source used or scan the image and display it through a projection unit
- Whiteboard, chalkboard, smart board, or chart tablet to write student responses
- One copy of each primary source used for each student
- One copy of the translation of the primary source used for each student

Primary Sources Used

To find this primary source on the Library of Congress Web site, do a search on the American Memory home page. Search for Ulysses S. Grant to Abraham Lincoln, Sunday, August 23, 1863 (raising black regiments in the South).

Preactivity

A document analysis can be done on this primary source. Follow the format for document analysis in chapter 2—Document Analysis. Document analysis tools can be found in the appendix.

Activity

The students will discuss and review the primary source. Lead the class in a discussion about the first time African Americans were allowed in the military. What do you think people in the South thought of this? What do you think the people in the North thought about it? After the discussion, the students will write a letter to Lincoln from the point of view of a former slave. The students can take the role of someone who wants to be enlisted or someone who does not want to be enlisted. This activity can be done after the preactivity or after this topic has been previously discussed from the textbook.

Procedure

(One class period)

1. Show the primary source on the projection device. Read through the transcription with the class. Lead the class in a discussion regarding the significance of Lincoln's decision to

allow former black slaves to enlist in the military. Discuss the possible feelings of people in the North and the South. How did former slaves feel about the decision?

2. After the discussion, each student will write a letter to Lincoln from the point of view of a former slave. This former slave can be for or against the decision of blacks enlisting the military. This former slave can be a new enlistee, if desired.

Extension

(One or two class periods)

The students can choose to do the following:

• Predict what happened next and draw conclusions about the situation.

• Write a letter to Lincoln from the point of view of a former slave owner opposed to the decision.

Evaluation

Did students participate in the class discussion?

Refer to the rubric on page 59 when evaluating the letter.

Rubric

	4	3	2	1
Sentences/ Paragraphs	Complete sentences. More than five well-written paragraphs.	Complete sentences without fragments or run-ons. Three to four well-written paragraphs.	Mostly complete sentences with only a few sentence errors. Only two paragraphs.	Letter contained many sentence fragments or run-on sentences. Incomplete paragraphs or only one paragraph.
Introduction and Closing	Introduction and closing are present.	Introduction and closing are present.	Introduction and closing are present.	Introduction and/or closing are missing.
Grammar and Spelling	No errors in grammar or spelling.	Only one to two errors in grammar and/or spelling.	Three to four errors in grammar and/or spelling.	More than four errors in grammar and/or spelling.
Length	The letter is sixteen or more sentences.	The letter is ten to fifteen sentences.	The letter is five to nine sentences.	The letter is less than five sentences.
Capitalization/ Punctuation	No errors in capitalization/ punctuation.	One to two errors in capitalization/ punctuation.	Three to four errors in capitalization/ punctuation.	More than four errors in capitalization/punctuation.
Content	Accurate information presented. No factual errors.	Mostly accurate information presented. No factual errors.	Mostly accurate information presented. A few factual errors.	Mostly accurate information presented. Several factual errors.

From *Abraham Lincoln and His Era: Using the American Memory Project to Teach with Primary Sources* by Bobbi Ireland. Santa Barbara, CA: Libraries Unlimited. Copyright © 2010.

Memo Written by Abraham Lincoln to His Cabinet

Written Document

Overview

Students will use a memo from Abraham Lincoln to his cabinet as a part of a time line. Lincoln felt as though he would not be reelected in the November election. He sealed the memo in an envelope and did not show his cabinet until after the election, in which he was reelected. The memo was written in 1864. The students will use prior knowledge and decoding skills in order to comprehend the document.

Objectives

After completing this lesson, the students will be able to:

Create a time line

Summarize what they have learned

Gain understanding of the terminology

Time Required

One or two thirty-minute class periods for discussion

Recommended Grade Level

Grades 4–8

Topics

Government, Abraham Lincoln

Era

Civil War and Reconstruction, 1861–1877 time period

Standards

McREL 4th Edition Standards and Benchmarks

Historical Understanding

Understands and knows how to analyze chronological relationships and patterns

Understands the historical perspective

Understands how the Industrial Revolution, increasing immigration, the rapid expansion of slavery, and the westward movement changed American lives and led to regional tensions

Language Arts

Uses viewing and strategies to understand and interpret visual media

Uses grammatical and mechanical conventions in written compositions

Uses reading skills and strategies to understand and interpret a variety of literary texts

Working with Others

Displays effective interpersonal communication skills

Preparation

Have the following materials ready before the lesson:

- Prepare an overhead transparency of the primary source used or scan the image and display it through a projection unit
- Whiteboard, chalkboard, smart board, or chart tablet to write student responses
- One copy of the primary source used for each student
- One copy of the translation of the primary source used for each student
- Paper

Primary Sources Used

To find this primary source on the Library of Congress Web site, do a search on the American Memory home page. Search for Abraham Lincoln, Tuesday, August 23, 1864 (memorandum on possibility of not being reelected; endorsed by members of the cabinet).

Preactivity

A document analysis can be done on this primary source. Follow the format for document analysis in chapter 2—Document Analysis. Document analysis tools can be found in the appendix.

Activity

The students will discuss and review the primary source. Lead the class in a discussion about Lincoln's fears of not being reelected. The students will create a time line showing events that happened leading up to Lincoln's reelection. The primary source can be used in the time line. This activity can be done after the preactivity or after this topic has been previously discussed from the textbook.

Procedure

(One class period)

1. Show the class the primary source on the projection device. Lead the class in the discussion about Lincoln's reelection and the events that led up to it. The primary source can be used in the time line.

2. Students will make a time line on a piece of paper. The time line should have a title and include important events that led up to Lincoln's reelection. When finished, each student will present his or her time line to the class. Display the time lines in the classroom or the hallway.

Extension

(One or two class periods)

The students can choose to do the following:

- Write a larger letter from Lincoln's point of view explaining why he thought he would not be reelected.

- Analyze why the president wrote the memo but sealed it and kept it from Congress. Why do you think he did not just talk to his cabinet?

- Predict what happened next and draw conclusions about the situation.

- Conduct an interview with one student being Lincoln and the other student being a television reporter/interviewer. Discuss Lincoln's feelings concerning the November election.

Evaluation

Did the student participate in the class discussion?

Refer to the rubric on page 63 for evaluation of time line. This rubric evaluates the preparation process as well as the final product. Be sure to observe and monitor students during the planning and actual work time.

Rubric

	4	3	2	1
Spelling/ Capitalization	Spelling and capitalization are correct.	Spelling and capitalization contained a few errors. Although student attempted to fix errors.	Spelling and capitalization contained many errors. Although student attempted to fix errors.	There were many spelling and capitalization errors. Student did not attempt to fix errors.
Content/Facts	Facts for all events on time line were accurate.	Facts for all events on time line were almost all accurate.	Facts for all events on time line were fairly accurate.	Facts for most all events on time line were inaccurate.
Readability	Appearance is nice and very easy to read.	Appearance of the time line is average and easy to read.	The time line is readable.	The time line is difficult to read.
Preparation	The student researched the events and made accurate notes before creating the time line.	The student researched the events and made somewhat accurate notes before creating the time line.	The student researched some of the events and made some notes before creating the time line.	The student did not research or create notes before creating the time line.
Resources	Nine to twelve events were included and all were related to the topic.	Six to eight events were included and all were related to the topic.	Four to five events were included and all were related to the topic.	Less than four events were included.
Dates	Accurate and complete dates included for each event.	Accurate and complete dates included for most events.	Accurate and complete dates included for some events.	Missing or incomplete dates throughout.
Title	Creative title appropriately placed on the time line.	Good title appropriately placed on the time line.	Title appropriately placed on the time line.	Missing title or inappropriately placed on the time line.

From *Abraham Lincoln and His Era: Using the American Memory Project to Teach with Primary Sources* by Bobbi Ireland. Santa Barbara, CA: Libraries Unlimited. Copyright © 2010.

Eyewitness Account of President Lincoln's Assassination

Written Document

Overview

The students will use an eyewitness account of Lincoln's assassination in the making of a multimedia presentation showing events in his life and ending with the assassination. The document was written in 1865. The students will use prior knowledge and decoding skills in order to comprehend the document.

Objectives

After completing this lesson, the students will be able to:

Create a multimedia presentation

Summarize what they have learned

Gain understanding of the terminology

Time Required

One or two thirty-minute class periods for discussion

Recommended Grade Level

Grades 4–8

Topics

Government, Abraham Lincoln

Era

Civil War and Reconstruction, 1861–1877 time period

Standards

McREL 4th Edition Standards and Benchmarks

Historical Understanding

Understands and knows how to analyze chronological relationships and patterns

Understands the historical perspective

Understands how the Industrial Revolution, increasing immigration, the rapid expansion of slavery, and the westward movement changed American lives and led to regional tensions

Language Arts

Uses viewing and strategies to understand and interpret visual media

Uses grammatical and mechanical conventions in written compositions

Uses reading skills and strategies to understand and interpret a variety of literary texts

Working with Others

Displays effective interpersonal communication skills

Preparation

Have the following materials ready before the lesson:

- Prepare an overhead transparency of the primary source used or scan the image and display it through a projection unit
- Whiteboard, chalkboard, smart board, or chart tablet to write student responses
- One copy of each primary source used for each student
- One copy of each translation of the primary sources used for each student

Primary Sources Used

To find this primary source on the Library of Congress Web site, do a search on the American Memory home page. Search for James S. Knox to Knox, Saturday, April 15, 1865 (eyewitness account of Lincoln's assassination).

Preactivity

A document analysis can be done on this primary source. Follow the format for document analysis in chapter 2—Document Analysis. Document analysis tools can be found in the appendix.

Activity

The students will discuss and review the primary source. The students will work in learning groups to create a multimedia presentation showing events in Lincoln's life and ending with the assassination. This activity can be done after the preactivity or after this topic has been previously discussed from the textbook.

Procedure

(One class period)

1. Show the primary source on the projection unit. Read the transcription while the students follow along. Lead the class in a discussion about his assassination. Discuss all the important events that happened in Lincoln's life.

2. Split the class up into learning groups. Each group will do research and create a multimedia presentation depicting major events in Lincoln's life and ending with his assassination.

Extension

(One or two class periods)

The students can choose to do the following:

- Write a letter from an eyewitness point of view of the assassination based on the facts you have.
- Analyze why someone would want to assassinate the president.
- Predict what happened next and draw conclusions about the situation.
- Conduct an interview with one student being an eyewitness to the assassination and the other student being a TV reporter/interviewer.

Evaluation

Refer to the rubric on page 67 when evaluating the multimedia presentation.

Rubric

	4	3	2	1
Background	Choice of background colors is excellent and eye-catching but not distracting.	Choice of background colors is good and eye-catching but not distracting.	Choice of background colors is eye-catching but somewhat distracting.	Choice of background colors is overwhelming and distracting.
Sounds	Great sounds are used. They add much to the overall feel of the presentation. Great volume level.	Great sounds are used. They add much to the overall feel of the presentation. Volume level could be adjusted (higher or lower).	Good sounds are used. More or less sounds could have been used. Volume level could be adjusted (higher or lower).	Sounds were not utilized appropriately in the presentation. Volume level needed adjustment (higher or lower).
Quality	Very good quality presentation. Unique and original.	Good quality presentation. Unique and original.	Good quality presentation. Could have been more unique and original.	Better quality of work needed. Lacked originality and uniqueness.
Text/Font	Font formats chosen wisely. Font, color, and size all worked to contribute to the overall presentation. Very easily read.	Font formats chosen well. Font, color, and size all worked to contribute to the overall presentation. Very easily read.	Font formats chosen could have been less. Font, color, and size seemed a little too much for the overall presentation. A little hard to read.	Too many font formats. Font, color, and size too much for the overall presentation. Very hard to read.
Content	Accurate information is presented in the presentation. No factual errors.	Mostly accurate information is presented in the presentation. No factual errors.	Mostly accurate information is presented in the presentation. A few factual errors.	Mostly accurate information is presented in the presentation. Several factual errors.
Sequencing	All information is in logical sequence. Very easy to follow.	Most information is in logical sequence. Easy to follow.	Information is not all in logical sequence. Not always easy to follow.	Information is not in logical sequence. Not easy to follow.
Effective	The presentation is very effective. A good understanding of the topic was achieved by the audience.	The presentation is effective. A good understanding of the topic was achieved by the audience.	The presentation is fairly effective. An understanding of the topic was not achieved by the audience.	The presentation is not effective. More parts could have been added. An understanding of the topic was not achieved by the audience.

From *Abraham Lincoln and His Era: Using the American Memory Project to Teach with Primary Sources* by Bobbi Ireland. Santa Barbara, CA: Libraries Unlimited. Copyright © 2010.

CHAPTER 4

Lesson Plans Incorporating the Arts and Humanities in Primary Sources

Poem Written by Abraham Lincoln

Arts and Humanities

Overview

Students will explain, discuss, and analyze a handwritten poem by Abraham Lincoln. The poem was written in 1846. The students will use prior knowledge and decoding skills in order to comprehend the document.

Objectives

After completing this lesson, the students will be able to:

Observe and analyze the document

Gain understanding of the terminology

Time Required

One or two thirty-minute class periods for discussion

Recommended Grade Level

Grades 4–8

Topics

Government, Abraham Lincoln

Era

National Expansion and Reform, 1815–1860

Standards

McREL 4th Edition Standards and Benchmarks

Historical Understanding

Understands and knows how to analyze chronological relationships and patterns

Understands the historical perspective

Understands how the Industrial Revolution, increasing immigration, the rapid expansion of slavery, and the westward movement changed American lives and led to regional tensions

Language Arts

Uses viewing and strategies to understand and interpret visual media

Uses grammatical and mechanical conventions in written compositions

Uses reading skills and strategies to understand and interpret a variety of literary texts

Working with Others

Displays effective interpersonal communication skills

Arts and Communication

Practice creativity: uses critical and creative thinking in various arts and communication settings

Role of culture: understands ways in which the human experience is transmitted and reflected in the arts and communication

Preparation

Have the following materials ready before the lesson:

- Prepare an overhead transparency of the primary source used or scan the image and display it through a projection unit
- Whiteboard, chalkboard, smart board, or chart tablet to write student responses
- One copy of the primary source used for each student
- One copy of the translation of the primary source used for each student

Primary Sources Used

To find this primary source on the Library of Congress Web site, do a search on the American Memory home page. Search for Abraham Lincoln, 1846 (poem, "My Child-hood Home I See Again).

Preactivity

A document analysis can be done on this primary source. Follow the format for document analysis in chapter 2—Document Analysis. Document analysis tools can be found in the appendix.

Activity

The students will discuss and review the primary source. Lead the class in a discussion about Lincoln. What kind of man was he? What did he feel strongly about? How do you think he felt about coming from a rural upbringing and ending up being president of the United States? The students will work in learning groups to analyze the handwritten poem and write an essay. This activity can be done after the preactivity or after this topic has been previously discussed from the textbook.

Procedure

(One class period)

1. When starting the activity, involve students in the lesson by asking discussion questions:

    What would it be like to visit your childhood home after being away for many years?

    Have you ever known someone who completely changed his or her personality?
    As the discussion expands, write responses and questions on the board or tablet.

2. On the overhead projector or projection device, show a large version of the primary source. Then give each student his or her own copy of the written document along with a transcription of it. Read the transcription to the students as they follow along or have them take turns reading the document aloud.

3. Split the class into learning groups to analyze the poem. On paper, the groups will describe the poem, find figurative language, and interpret what they feel the poem means.

Extension

(One or two class periods)

The students can choose to do the following:

- Write a poem describing where you grew up.

- Analyze why Lincoln might feel sad when thinking about old memories.

- Create a multimedia presentation that shows where you have grown up.

- Be a storyteller and retell Abraham's poem in your own words.

- Design a brochure telling Lincoln about the place you live (town, city, or neighborhood) to encourage others to visit the area.

Evaluation

Refer to the rubric on page 72 when evaluating the essay about the poem.

Rubric

	4	3	2	1
Description	Gives a complete and detailed description of the subject matter in the poem.	Gives a complete and detailed description of most of the subject matter in the poem.	Gives a complete and detailed description of some of the subject matter in the poem.	Descriptions are lacking and are incomplete.
Analysis	Accurately describes ideas and figurative language in the poem and can identify the theme, meaning, mood, or feelings in the poem.	Accurately describes some ideas and figurative language in the poem and can identify the theme, meaning, mood, or feelings in the poem.	Accurately describes some ideas and figurative language in the poem but cannot identify the theme, meaning, mood, or feelings in the poem.	Did not describe ideas and figurative language and did not identify any other elements of the poem.
Interpretation	Finds the symbolic or metaphorical meaning in the poem and is able to show examples from the poem.	Finds the symbolic or metaphorical meaning in some of the poem and is able to show examples from the poem.	Student is able to find areas in the poem that reflect Abraham Lincoln's feelings.	Does not interpret the poem in any way.

From *Abraham Lincoln and His Era: Using the American Memory Project to Teach with Primary Sources* by Bobbi Ireland. Santa Barbara, CA: Libraries Unlimited. Copyright © 2010.

Certificate of Membership Given to Abraham Lincoln

Arts and Humanities

Overview

A logo or advertisement will be created after discussing a certificate of membership that was given to Abraham Lincoln in 1860. The students will use prior knowledge and decoding skills in order to comprehend the document.

Objectives

After completing this lesson, the students will be able to:

Observe and analyze the primary source

Summarize what they have learned

Gain understanding of the terminology

Time Required

One or two thirty-minute class periods for discussion

Recommended Grade Level

Grades 4–8

Topics

Government, Abraham Lincoln

Era

National Expansion and Reform, 1815–1860

Standards

McREL 4th Edition Standards and Benchmarks

Historical Understanding

Understands and knows how to analyze chronological relationships and patterns

Understands the historical perspective

Language Arts

Uses viewing and strategies to understand and interpret visual media

Uses grammatical and mechanical conventions in written compositions

Uses reading skills and strategies to understand and interpret a variety of literary texts

Working with Others

Displays effective interpersonal communication skills

Arts and Communication

Aesthetic experiences: Understands the principles, processes, and products associated with arts and communication media

Knows and applies appropriate criteria to arts and communication products

Visual Arts

Understands the visual arts in relation to history and cultures

Preparation

Have the following materials ready before the lesson:

- Prepare an overhead transparency of the primary source used or scan the image and display it through a projection unit
- Whiteboard, chalkboard, smart board, or chart tablet to write student responses
- One copy of the primary source used for each student
- One copy of the translation of the primary source used for each student

Primary Sources Used

To find this primary source on the Library of Congress Web site, do a search on the American Memory home page. Search for: Chicago Wide-Awake Republican Club to Abraham Lincoln, Friday, June 1, 1860 (Certificate of membership).

Preactivity

A document analysis can be done on this primary source. Follow the format for document analysis in chapter 2—Document Analysis. Document analysis tools can be found in the appendix.

Analysis Tool

Poster analysis form

Activity

The students will discuss and review the primary source. Discuss certificates, logos, and advertisement. What makes all these things stand out? Discuss the importance of design quality and creativity. The students will create a logo or advertisement for a company using pictures and symbols associated with Lincoln's face, shadow, log cabin, or any other significant image. This activity can be done after the preactivity or after this topic has been previously discussed from the textbook.

Procedure

(One class period)

1. The students will work in learning groups to create a logo or advisement using symbols associated with Lincoln. This logo or advertisement can be for any type of store or company. Encourage the students to be creative. For example, you could have the motto "Lincoln's General Store: Where a Penny Can Buy Something" and a picture of a penny is used in the logo.

2. After logos or advertisements are created, the learning groups will present them orally to the class. After the presentation, display the designs in the classroom or the hallway.

Extension

(One or two class periods)

The students can choose to do the following:

• Create a certificate for Lincoln (an achievement certificate or a special citizenship award).

• Write a letter from Lincoln back to the organization that gave him the certificate expressing his gratitude.

Evaluation

Refer to the rubric on page 76 when evaluating the project. This is a product and process rubric. Be sure to observe and monitor students during the planning and actual working time during the project.

Rubric

	4	3	2	1
Planning/ Organization	Took adequate time in planning and organizing the design.	Took some time in planning and organizing the design but had to be reminded to continue working.	Took a fair amount of time in planning and organizing the design. Needed several reminders to continue working.	Went right into designing without any preplanning or organization.
Thematic Accuracy	The student's design fits into the theme of the assignment perfectly.	The student's design fits into the theme of the assignment well.	Portions of the student's design fits into the theme of the assignment.	The student's design does not fit into the theme of the assignment.
Color	The colors in the design work well together.	The colors in the design work good together.	The colors in the design work well together but more or fewer colors could have been used.	The colors in the design do not coordinate together or work for the overall presentation.
Time/Effort	Used time wisely. The student took the assignment seriously.	Used time wisely. The student took the assignment fairly seriously.	Did not always use time wisely. The student did not always take the assignment seriously.	Time not used wisely. Student did not take the assignment seriously.

From *Abraham Lincoln and His Era: Using the American Memory Project to Teach with Primary Sources* by Bobbi Ireland. Santa Barbara, CA: Libraries Unlimited. Copyright © 2010.

Photographs of Abraham Lincoln

Arts and Humanities

Overview
This is an analysis of photographs of Abraham Lincoln over the years spanning his journey from the U.S. Congress to the office of president.

Objectives
After completing this lesson, the students will be able to:

Observe and analyze the photographs

Summarize what they have learned

Time Required
One or two thirty-minute class periods for discussion

Recommended Grade Level
Grades 4–8

Topics
Government, Abraham Lincoln

Era
National Expansion and Reform, 1815–1860

Standards
McREL 4th Edition Standards and Benchmarks

Historical Understanding
Understands and knows how to analyze chronological relationships and patterns

Understands the historical perspective

Language Arts
Uses viewing and strategies to understand and interpret visual media

Uses grammatical and mechanical conventions in written compositions

Uses reading skills and strategies to understand and interpret a variety of literary texts

Working with Others

Displays effective interpersonal communication skills

Preparation

Have the following materials ready before the lesson:

• Prepare an overhead transparency of the primary sources used or scan the images and display them through a projection unit

• Whiteboard, chalkboard, smart board, or chart tablet to write student responses

• One copy of each primary source used for each student

Primary Sources Used

To find these primary sources on the Library of Congress Web site, do a search on the American Memory home page. Search for: Abraham Lincoln photographs. Choose three to six photographs that show the sequence of an aging Lincoln.

Preactivity

A document analysis can be done on this primary source. Follow the format for document analysis in chapter 2—Document Analysis. Document analysis tools can be found in the appendix.

Activity

The students will discuss and review the primary sources. Lead the class in a discussion about the physical differences in the photographs of Lincoln. This activity can be done after the preactivity or after this topic has been previously discussed from the textbook.

Procedure

(One class period)

1. When starting the activity, get students involved in the lesson by asking discussion questions:

    How have you or your friends changed since kindergarten?

    How have you changed over the past five years?

    As the discussion expands, write responses and questions on the board or tablet.

2. On the overhead projector or projection device, show a large version of one of the photographs. One by one, show the next photographs of Lincoln. Then give each student his or her own copy of the photographs.

3. The students will choose two photographs to create an essay around. The students will compare and contrast the two photographs in a written format. The essay should include physical characteristics that were apparent and the student's opinion on why the changes happened. The student should research the dates the photographs were taken and include important events that happened when the photograph was taken. The essays will be presented orally to the class.

Extension

(One or two class periods)

The students can choose to do the following:

- Use the photographs and drawings to create a time line.

- Write a letter, as Lincoln, reflecting on how he had changed, both physically and mentally, over the years. (This activity will require the student to do further research on the subject and will take additional time.)

- Make a multimedia presentation of Lincoln's life. Show the physical changes in Lincoln. Include important events that happened when the photographs were taken.

Evaluation

Refer to the rubric on page 80 when evaluating the essay.

Rubric

	4	3	2	1
Sentences/ Paragraphs	Complete sentences. Five or more well-written paragraphs.	Complete sentences without fragments or run-ons. Three to four well-written paragraphs.	Mostly complete sentences with only a few sentence errors. Only two paragraphs.	Letter contained many sentence fragments or run-on sentences. Incomplete paragraphs or only one paragraph.
Introduction and Closing	Introduction and closing are present.	Introduction and closing are present.	Introduction and closing are present.	Introduction and/or closing are missing.
Grammar and Spelling	No errors in grammar or spelling.	Only one or two errors in grammar and/or spelling.	Three to four errors in grammar and/or spelling	More than four errors in grammar and/or spelling.
Ideas	Clear and organized ideas. Essay is easy to follow and understand. Included much historical information.	Relatively clear and organized ideas. Essay is easy to follow and understand. Included some historical information.	Somewhat clear and organized ideas. Essay is not easy to follow and understand.	Unclear and disorganized ideas. Essay is very hard to follow and understand.
Capitalization/ Punctuation	No errors in capitalization/ punctuation.	One to two errors in capitalization/ punctuation.	Three to four errors in capitalization/ punctuation.	More than four errors in capitalization/ punctuation.
Neatness	Essay is typed and neat.	Essay is neatly hand-written.	Essay is typed but messy and maybe crinkled.	Essay is typed but the actual condition of the paper is a mess.
Content	Accurate information is presented in the presentation. No factual errors.	Mostly accurate information is presented in the presentation. No factual errors.	Mostly accurate information is presented in the presentation. A few factual errors.	Mostly accurate information is presented in the presentation. Several factual errors.

From *Abraham Lincoln and His Era: Using the American Memory Project to Teach with Primary Sources* by Bobbi Ireland. Santa Barbara, CA: Libraries Unlimited. Copyright © 2010.

Painting by Thomas Nast

Arts and Humanities

Overview

This is an analysis of a painting by Thomas Nast showing the emancipation of slaves after the end of the Civil War.

Objectives

After completing this lesson, the students will be able to:

Observe and analyze the painting

Summarize what they have learned from the painting

Understand the significance of the painting

Time Required

One or two thirty-minute class periods for discussion

Recommended Grade Level

Grades 4–8

Topics

Government, Abraham Lincoln

Era

Civil War and Reconstruction, 1861–1877 time period

Standards

McREL 4th Edition Standards and Benchmarks

Historical Understanding

Understands and knows how to analyze chronological relationships and patterns

Understands the historical perspective

Understands how the Industrial Revolution, increasing immigration, the rapid expansion of slavery, and the westward movement changed American lives and led to regional tensions

Language Arts

Uses viewing and strategies to understand and interpret visual media

Uses grammatical and mechanical conventions in written compositions

Uses reading skills and strategies to understand and interpret a variety of literary texts

Working with Others

Displays effective interpersonal communication skills

Preparation

Have the following materials ready before the lesson:

- Prepare an overhead transparency of the primary source used or scan the image and display it through a projection unit.
- Show the students only parts of the painting at a time.
- Scan parts of the painting or cover up parts when showing the students.
- Whiteboard, chalkboard, smart board, or chart tablet are used to write student responses
- One copy of each primary source is used for each student.

Primary Sources Used

To find this primary source on the Library of Congress Web site, do a search on the American Memory home page. Search for emancipation.

Preactivity

A document analysis can be done on this primary source. Follow the format for document analysis in chapter 2—Document Analysis. Document analysis tools can be found in the appendix.

Activity

The students will be looking at only parts of the painting at a time. When finished, the students will write an essay summarizing and explaining the significance of the painting. This activity can be done after the preactivity or after this topic has been previously discussed from the textbook.

Primary Source Analysis Tool

Painting analysis form

Procedure

(One class period)

1. Introduce the primary source to the class. Give each student the primary source analysis tool. Explain that they will be using the handout to analyze the painting. Explain that parts of the painting will be covered up. Students will only see small parts of the painting at a time. On the overhead projector or projection device, show a large version of the painting. Be sure to cover up parts of the painting. Don't give the students the copy of the painting until the entire painting has been revealed.

2. Go through the analysis tool with the class. As the discussion expands, write responses and questions on the board or tablet. Encourage the students to closely examine the parts of the painting. Reveal parts of the painting. When the entire painting is shown, the students will write an essay that summarizes the painting and the analysis.

Extension

(One or two class periods)

The students can choose to do the following:

• Write a paragraph describing what is happening in one part of the painting.

• Create a picture collage of the significant events in Lincoln's life and end with emancipation.

• Be a storyteller. Tell the class the story of the slaves, Lincoln, and the emancipation.

Evaluation

Refer to the rubric on page 84 for evaluation on the essay.

Assess the primary source analysis tool for evidence that the students understood how to do the analysis.

Rubric

	4	3	2	1
Sentences/ Paragraphs	Complete sentences. More than five well-written paragraphs.	Complete sentences without fragments or run-ons. Three to four well-written paragraphs.	Mostly complete sentences with only a few sentence errors. Only two paragraphs.	Letter contained many sentence fragments or run-on sentences. Incomplete paragraphs or only one paragraph.
Introduction and Closing	Introduction and closing are present.	Introduction and closing are present.	Introduction and closing are present.	Introduction and/or closing are missing.
Grammar and Spelling	No errors in grammar or spelling.	Only one or two errors in grammar and/or spelling.	Three to four errors in grammar and/or spelling.	More than four errors in grammar and/or spelling.
Ideas	Clear and organized ideas. Essay easy to follow and understand. Included much historical information.	Relatively clear and organized ideas. Essay easy to follow and understand. Included some historical information.	Somewhat clear and organized ideas. Essay was not easy to follow and understand.	Unclear and disorganized ideas. Essay very hard to follow and understand.
Capitalization/ Punctuation	No errors in capitalization/ punctuation.	One or two errors in capitalization/ punctuation.	Three to four errors in capitalization/ punctuation.	More than four errors in capitalization/ punctuation.
Neatness	Essay is typed and neat.	Essay is neatly hand-written.	Essay is typed but messy and maybe crinkled.	Essay is typed but the actual condition of the paper is a mess.
Content	Accurate information is presented. No factual errors.	Mostly accurate information is presented. No factual errors.	Mostly accurate information is presented. A few factual errors.	Mostly accurate information is presented. Several factual errors.

From *Abraham Lincoln and His Era: Using the American Memory Project to Teach with Primary Sources* by Bobbi Ireland. Santa Barbara, CA: Libraries Unlimited. Copyright © 2010.

Painting Showing the Assassination of President Lincoln

Arts and Humanities

Overview

An analysis of a painting that shows the assassination of Lincoln at Ford's Theatre, Washington, D.C., April 14, 1865.

Objectives

After completing this lesson, the students will be able to:

Observe and analyze the painting

Summarize what they have learned from the painting

Time Required

One or two thirty-minute class periods for discussion

Recommended Grade Level

Grades 4–8

Topics

Government, Abraham Lincoln

Era

Civil War and Reconstruction, 1861–1877 time period

Standards

McREL 4th Edition Standards and Benchmarks

Historical Understanding

Understands and knows how to analyze chronological relationships and patterns

Understands the historical perspective

Understands how the Industrial Revolution, increasing immigration, the rapid expansion of slavery, and the westward movement changed American lives and led to regional tensions

Language Arts

Uses viewing and strategies to understand and interpret visual media

Uses grammatical and mechanical conventions in written compositions

Uses reading skills and strategies to understand and interpret a variety of literary texts

Working with Others

Displays effective interpersonal communication skills

Preparation

Have the following materials ready before the lesson:

- Prepare an overhead transparency of the primary source used or scan the image and display it through a projection unit

- Whiteboard, chalkboard, smart board, or chart tablet to write student responses

- One copy of each primary source used for each student

Primary Sources Used

To find this primary source on the Library of Congress Web site, do a search on the American Memory home page. Search for the assassination of President Lincoln at Ford's Theatre, Washington, D.C., April 14, 1865.

Preactivity

A document analysis can be done on this primary source. Follow the format for document analysis in chapter 2—Document Analysis. Document analysis tools can be found in the appendix.

Activity

The students will summarize what is seen in the painting by using only one word. Write the word on a sheet of paper and decorate and style as needed to add to the summarizing. When finished, students will orally present their work to the class. This activity can be done after the preactivity or after this topic has been previously discussed from the textbook

Procedure

(One class period)

1. Show the primary source to the class. Lead the class in a discussion about the painting. What was the artist trying to express? What feelings are present in the painting?

2. Explain to the students that they will be choosing one word to represent the content in the painting. The students will write the word on paper and decorate the paper with pictures that help to represent the content in the painting.

Extension

(One or two class periods)

The students can choose to do the following:

• Write an essay describing what is happening in the painting.

• Retell the painting describing the detail. Orally present it to the class.

• Work with a group of students and write scripts for Reader's Theatre based on the painting. Then perform it for the class.

Evaluation

Use the rubric on page 88 to evaluate the project. This rubric is both a process and a project rubric. Be sure to observe the students while the project is in both the planning and the development stages.

Rubric

	4	3	2	1
Planning/ Organization	Took adequate time in planning and organizing the design.	Took some time in planning and organizing the design. But had to be reminded to continue working.	Took a fair amount of time in planning and organizing the design. Needed several reminders to continue working.	Went right into designing without any preplanning or organization.
Thematic Accuracy	The student's design fits into the theme of the assignment perfectly.	The student's design fits into the theme of the assignment well.	Portions of the student's design fit into the theme of the assignment.	The student's design does not fit into the theme of the assignment.
Color	The colors in the design work well together.	The colors in the design work well together.	The colors in the design work well together but more/less colors could have been used.	The colors in the design do not coordinate together or work for the overall presentation.
Time/Effort	Used time wisely. The student took the assignment seriously.	Used time wisely. The student took the assignment fairly seriously.	Did not always use time wisely. The student did not always take the assignment seriously.	Time not used wisely. Student did not take the assignment seriously.
Content	Accurate information is presented. No factual errors.	Mostly accurate information is presented. No factual errors.	Mostly accurate information is presented. A few factual errors.	Mostly accurate information is presented. Several factual errors.

From *Abraham Lincoln and His Era: Using the American Memory Project to Teach with Primary Sources* by Bobbi Ireland. Santa Barbara, CA: Libraries Unlimited. Copyright © 2010.

Reward Posters

Arts and Humanities

Overview

This is an analysis of reward posters that were used after the assassination of Abraham Lincoln. The students will use prior knowledge and decoding skills in order to comprehend the document.

Objectives

After completing this lesson, the students will be able to:

Observe and analyze the posters

Summarize what they have learned from the posters

Understand the significance of the posters

Time Required

One or two thirty-minute class periods for discussion

Recommended Grade Level

Grades 4–8

Topics

Government, Abraham Lincoln

Era

Civil War and Reconstruction, 1861–1877 time period

Standards

McREL 4th Edition Standards and Benchmarks

Historical Understanding

Understands and knows how to analyze chronological relationships and patterns

Understands the historical perspective

Understands how the Industrial Revolution, increasing immigration, the rapid expansion of slavery, and the westward movement changed American lives and led to regional tensions

Language Arts

Uses viewing and strategies to understand and interpret visual media

Uses grammatical and mechanical conventions in written compositions

Uses reading skills and strategies to understand and interpret a variety of literary texts

Working with Others

Displays effective interpersonal communication skills

Preparation

Have the following materials ready before the lesson:

- Prepare an overhead transparency of the primary source used or scan the images and display them through a projection unit
- Whiteboard, chalkboard, smart board, or chart tablet to write student responses
- One copy of each primary source used for each student

Primary Sources Used

To find this primary source on the Library of Congress Web site, do a search on the American Memory home page. Search for (1) $100,000 reward! The murderer of our late beloved president, Abraham Lincoln, is still at large, The Alfred Whital Stern Collection of Lincolniana, and (2) 100,000 reward! The murderer of our late beloved president, Abraham Lincoln, is still at large.

Preactivity

A document analysis can be done on the primary sources. Follow the format for document analysis in chapter 2—Document Analysis. Document analysis tools can be found in the appendix.

Activity

The students will design and create a reward poster. This activity can be done after the preactivity or after this topic has been previously discussed from the textbook.

Primary Source Analysis Tool

Poster analysis form

Procedure

(One class period)

1. Show the primary sources on a projection device to the class.
2. Lead the class in a discussion about the two reward posters. What is liked and disliked about the posters?
3. The students will use information from the actual reward posters to create their own reward poster. When finished, display the reward posters in the classroom or other location.

Extension

(One or two class periods)

The students can choose to do the following:

- Write a paragraph describing the posters.
- Create a collage of the significant events in Lincoln's life.
- Compare and contrast the two reward posters.
- Research the amount of reward money into today's terms. How much money would $100,000 in 1865 be worth today?

Evaluation

Use the rubric on page 92 to evaluate the reward poster. The rubric contains process and project assessments. Be sure to observe the students during both the planning and the working stages of the project.

Rubric

	4	3	2	1
Planning/ Organization	Took adequate time in planning and organizing the design.	Took some time in planning and organizing the design but had to be reminded to continue working.	Took a fair amount of time in planning and organizing the design. Needed several reminders to continue working.	Went right into designing without any preplanning or organization.
Thematic Accuracy	The student's design fits into the theme of the assignment perfectly.	The student's design fits into the theme of the assignment well.	Portions of the student's design fit into the theme of the assignment.	The student's design does not fit into the theme of the assignment.
Color	The colors in the design work well together.	The colors in the design work well together.	The colors in the design work well together but more/less colors could have been used.	The colors in the design do not coordinate together or work for the overall presentation.
Time/Effort	Used time wisely. The student took the assignment seriously.	Used time wisely. The student took the assignment fairly seriously.	Did not always use time wisely. The student did not always take the assignment seriously.	Time not used wisely. Student did not take the assignment seriously.
Content	Accurate information is presented. No factual errors.	Mostly accurate information is presented. No factual errors.	Mostly accurate information is presented. A few factual errors.	Mostly accurate information is presented. Several factual errors.

From *Abraham Lincoln and His Era: Using the American Memory Project to Teach with Primary Sources* by Bobbi Ireland. Santa Barbara, CA: Libraries Unlimited. Copyright © 2010.

Iron Casts Made of Abraham Lincoln's Hands

Arts and Humanities

Overview

This is an analysis of iron casts that were made of Lincoln's hands. Lincoln said he shook so many hands that his hand was swollen. A cast was made to show the difference, in size, of his hands.

Objectives

After completing this lesson, the students will be able to:

Observe and analyze the picture of the iron casts

Time Required

One or two thirty-minute class periods for discussion

Recommended Grade Level

Grades 4–8

Topics

Government, Abraham Lincoln

Era

Civil War and Reconstruction, 1861–1877 time period

Standards

McREL 4th Edition Standards and Benchmarks

Historical Understanding

Understands and knows how to analyze chronological relationships and patterns

Understands the historical perspective

Understands how the Industrial Revolution, increasing immigration, the rapid expansion of slavery, and the westward movement changed American lives and led to regional tensions

Language Arts

Uses viewing and strategies to understand and interpret visual media

Uses grammatical and mechanical conventions in written compositions

Uses reading skills and strategies to understand and interpret a variety of literary texts

Working with Others

Displays effective interpersonal communication skills

Preparation

Have the following materials ready before the lesson:

- Prepare an overhead transparency of the primary source used or scan the image and display it through a projection unit
- Whiteboard, chalkboard, smart board, or chart tablet to write student responses
- One copy of each primary source used for each student
- One copy of the analysis tool used for each student

Primary Sources Used

To find this primary source on the Library of Congress Web site, do a search on the American Memory home page. Search for the cast of Lincoln's hands lying on a plain backdrop, the image showing deep shadows on one side of the hands.

Preactivity

Another document analysis can be done on this primary source. Follow the format for document analysis in chapter 2—Document Analysis. Document analysis tools can be found in the appendix.

Activity

The students will be analyzing the casts of Lincoln's hands. This activity can be done after the preactivity or after this topic has been previously discussed from the textbook.

Primary Source Analysis Tool

Poster analysis form (even though this is not a poster, it can be used for discussion and analysis).

Procedure

(One class period)

1. Show the class the primary source. Have the students speculate on what it is. Have the class choose an investigative question. Once the class has picked an appropriate investigative question, write it on the board, paper, or smart board.
2. Give each student the primary source analysis tool. Explain to them that they will be using the handout to analyze the picture.
3. Go through the analysis tool with the class. As the discussion expands, write responses and questions on the board or tablet. Encourage the students to closely examine the primary

source. Lead your class into discussion so that their investigative question is answered. Some things to consider and ask when doing this type of analysis:

Why did the artist make a cast of his hands?

When were the casts created?

What are the casts showing?

Extension

(One or two class periods)

The students can choose to do the following:

• Write a paragraph describing what it would be like to shake hands for hours.

• Retell the experience of the castings by using Lincoln's point of view (additional research on the topic is required by the student).

• Create a model of hands with clay. Describe them to the class.

Evaluation

Refer to the document analysis tool for evaluation of the activity. Teacher observation of students' participation during the discussion can be noted as well.

Appendix: Analysis Tools

Cartoon

Look at the cartoon and list any of the following you see:		
	Title	
	Objects/People	
	Words/Phrases	
	Dates/Numbers	
Sensory Qualities		
	Are lines bold, fussy, light, hard or soft?	

Look Closer...

Images		
	Which objects are used as symbols?	
	Why were the symbols used and what do they represent?	
	Is anything exaggerated? How?	
	Is the cartoon realistic or abstract?	

From Eastern Illinois University Teaching with Primary Sources (www.eiu.edu/~eiutps/), 2009. Reprinted with permission in *Abraham Lincoln and His Era: Using the American Memory Project to Teach with Primary Sources* by Bobbi Ireland. Santa Barbara, CA: Libraries Unlimited. Copyright © 2010.

| | List adjectives that describe emotions visible in the cartoon. | |

Words

| | Which words or phrases appear to be important? Why? | |

Cartoon Purpose

Describe the action taking place in the cartoon.

Explain how the words in the cartoon explain the symbols.

What is the message of the cartoon?

Who are the people who might agree with the cartoon? What might be the public's reaction to this cartoon?

From Eastern Illinois University Teaching with Primary Sources (www.eiu.edu/~eiutps/), 2009. Reprinted with permission in *Abraham Lincoln and His Era: Using the American Memory Project to Teach with Primary Sources* by Bobbi Ireland. Santa Barbara, CA: Libraries Unlimited. Copyright © 2010.

Letter

First Reading

On your copy of the letter:

Circle the date the letter was written.

<u>Underline</u> words you don't recognize or can't read.

Look at the letter:

Who was the letter written to?

Who wrote the letter?

From the salutation, do they appear to know each other?

Read the letter:

Go back and write in words that you think make sense for those that you underlined.

Choose one sentence from the letter and rewrite it here:

What about this sentence attracted your attention?

What do you think this letter is about?

From Eastern Illinois University Teaching with Primary Sources (www.eiu.edu/~eiutps/), 2009. Reprinted with permission in *Abraham Lincoln and His Era: Using the American Memory Project to Teach with Primary Sources* by Bobbi Ireland. Santa Barbara, CA: Libraries Unlimited. Copyright © 2010.

After Reading a Transcript or Listening to a Reading of the Letter:

What new information do you have about the letter?

How accurate was the sentence you wrote?

Why do you think the author wrote this letter?

Why do you think someone saved this letter?

What questions do you have about this letter?

How can you learn the answers to your questions?

From Eastern Illinois University Teaching with Primary Sources (www.eiu.edu/~eiutps/), 2009. Reprinted with permission in *Abraham Lincoln and His Era: Using the American Memory Project to Teach with Primary Sources* by Bobbi Ireland. Santa Barbara, CA: Libraries Unlimited. Copyright © 2010.

Map

Title of Map
Check the circle(s) besides the type of map that describes the map you have.
• Raised relief map   • Political map   • Military map   • Topographic map   • Contour-line map   • Birds-eye view   • Natural resource map   • Artifact map   • Satellite photograph/mosaic   • Other   • Weather map   • Pictograph
Check the circle(s) besides the map parts that are visible on the map you have.
• Compass   • Date   • Scale   • Handwritten   • Notations   • Name of mapmaker   • Other   • Legend (key)   • Title
Date of the map
Creator of the map
Where was the map produced?

From Eastern Illinois University Teaching with Primary Sources (www.eiu.edu/~eiutps/), 2009. Reprinted with permission in *Abraham Lincoln and His Era: Using the American Memory Project to Teach with Primary Sources* by Bobbi Ireland. Santa Barbara, CA: Libraries Unlimited. Copyright © 2010.

Map Information
What natural landmarks and things do you notice on this map?
What man-made landmarks and things do you notice on this map?
List three things on this map that you think are important.
1. 2. 3.
Why do you think this map was created?
What evidence on the map suggests this?
What new information did you learn from this map?
Write a question to the mapmaker that is left unanswered by this map.

From Eastern Illinois University Teaching with Primary Sources (www.eiu.edu/~eiutps/), 2009. Reprinted with permission in *Abraham Lincoln and His Era: Using the American Memory Project to Teach with Primary Sources* by Bobbi Ireland. Santa Barbara, CA: Libraries Unlimited. Copyright © 2010.

Photo: The More You Look the More You See

What I see
Describe exactly what you see in the photo. What people and objects are shown? How are they arranged? What is the physical setting? What other details can you see?
What I Infer (Deduction)
Summarize what you already know about the situation and time period shown and people and objects that appear.

From Eastern Illinois University Teaching with Primary Sources (www.eiu.edu/~eiutps/), 2009. Reprinted with permission in *Abraham Lincoln and His Era: Using the American Memory Project to Teach with Primary Sources* by Bobbi Ireland. Santa Barbara, CA: Libraries Unlimited. Copyright © 2010.

Interpretation

Write what you conclude from what you see.

What is going on in the picture? Who are the people and what are they doing? What might be the function of the objects? What can we conclude about the time period?

Why do you believe the photo was taken?

Why do you believe this photo was saved?

What I Need to Investigate

What are three questions you have about the photo?

1.
2.
3.

Where can you research the answers to your questions?

Motion Picture

Before Viewing

Bibliographical Information

    Title of film

    Date created

    Filmmaker

Based on what you already know, what do you think we will see in this motion picture?

List three concepts or ideas that you might see and any people that you might see based on the title of the film.

Concepts/Ideas	People
1.	1.
2.	2.
3.	3.

While Viewing

Type of motion picture (may be more than one)

- Animated cartoon
- Newsreel
- Theatrical film
- Combat film
- Documentary film
- Propaganda film
- Training film
- Other

From Eastern Illinois University Teaching with Primary Sources (www.eiu.edu/~eiutps/), 2009. Reprinted with permission in *Abraham Lincoln and His Era: Using the American Memory Project to Teach with Primary Sources* by Bobbi Ireland. Santa Barbara, CA: Libraries Unlimited. Copyright © 2010.

Parts of the motion picture (may be more than one)

- Music
- Special effects
- Live action
- Animation
- Narration
- Color
- Background noise
- Dramatization

How do camera angles, lighting, music, narration, and editing contribute to the mood of the film? What is the mood or tone of the film?

After Viewing

Circle the things that you listed in the previewing activity that were in the motion picture.

What is the central message or messages of this motion picture?

Was the motion picture effective in communicating its message? How?

How do you think the filmmakers wanted viewers to respond?

Why do you believe this motion picture was made?

Write a question to the filmmaker that is left unanswered by the motion picture.

From Eastern Illinois University Teaching with Primary Sources (www.eiu.edu/~eiutps/), 2009. Reprinted with permission in *Abraham Lincoln and His Era: Using the American Memory Project to Teach with Primary Sources* by Bobbi Ireland. Santa Barbara, CA: Libraries Unlimited. Copyright © 2010.

Poem

Looking at the Poem

Look at the physical format and graphical elements. What do you see?

    Title

    Author

    Date created

    Does the look of the poem mean anything?

First Reading

Circle words that you don't know.

Highlight words or phrases that you think are expressive. What about the language appeals to you?

Write any important words that are used more than three times below.

Responding to the Poem

What are your personal reactions to the poem?

Underline your favorite line. Why did it capture your attention?

Why is this considered a poem?

From Eastern Illinois University Teaching with Primary Sources (www.eiu.edu/~eiutps/), 2009. Reprinted with permission in *Abraham Lincoln and His Era: Using the American Memory Project to Teach with Primary Sources* by Bobbi Ireland. Santa Barbara, CA: Libraries Unlimited. Copyright © 2010.

Thinking about History

For what audience was this poem written?

Why do you think the poet wrote this poem? What clues do you find that support this?

What does this poem tell you about life during this period in history?

Is the poem effective in communicating its message? How?

Write a question to the creator that is left unanswered by the poem.

What more do you want to know and how can you find out?

From Eastern Illinois University Teaching with Primary Sources (www.eiu.edu/~eiutps/), 2009. Reprinted with permission in *Abraham Lincoln and His Era: Using the American Memory Project to Teach with Primary Sources* by Bobbi Ireland. Santa Barbara, CA: Libraries Unlimited. Copyright © 2010.

Poster

First Glance

Looking at the poster, identify

The title

What emotions did you feel when you first saw the poster?

Symbolism

People

Person or character used   What do they symbolize?

Objects

Items used   What do they symbolize?

Colors

Colors used   What do they symbolize?

The Message

Are the messages in the poster primarily visual, verbal, or both? How?

Who do you think was the intended audience for this poster?

From Eastern Illinois University Teaching with Primary Sources (www.eiu.edu/~eiutps/), 2009. Reprinted with permission in *Abraham Lincoln and His Era: Using the American Memory Project to Teach with Primary Sources* by Bobbi Ireland. Santa Barbara, CA: Libraries Unlimited. Copyright © 2010.

110 Appendix

What do you think the creator hoped that people would do after seeing this poster?

After Viewing

The most effective posters use symbols that are simple, attract your attention, and are direct. Is this an effective poster? Why or why not?

List three things that you infer from this poster.

1.

2.

3.

Photo: Put Yourself in the Picture

Imagine Yourself in the Image Provided and List Three to Five Phrases Describing What You See, Hear, Taste, Touch, and Smell.

Sight: What do you see? People? Words? Buildings? Animals? Interesting items? Do these things give you clues about this time and place?

1.

2.

3.

4.

5.

Sound: What do you hear? People? Animals? Nature? Sounds from inside or outside of buildings? Sounds can indicate something good, bad, or sad.

1.

2.

3.

4.

5.

Taste: What do you taste? Are things edible or is there "something in the air"?

1.

2.

From Eastern Illinois University Teaching with Primary Sources (www.eiu.edu/~eiutps/), 2009. Reprinted with permission in *Abraham Lincoln and His Era: Using the American Memory Project to Teach with Primary Sources* by Bobbi Ireland. Santa Barbara, CA: Libraries Unlimited. Copyright © 2010.

3.

4.

5.

Smell: What smells are around you? City or rural scents? People? Animals? Businesses? Do they make you think of something good or bad?

1.

2.

3.

4.

5.

Touch: How and what do you feel? What is the environment like? Hot? Cold? Wet? Are there "things" that you can touch? What do they feel like?

1.

2.

3.

4.

5.

From Eastern Illinois University Teaching with Primary Sources (www.eiu.edu/~eiutps/), 2009. Reprinted with permission in *Abraham Lincoln and His Era: Using the American Memory Project to Teach with Primary Sources* by Bobbi Ireland. Santa Barbara, CA: Libraries Unlimited. Copyright © 2010.

Sheet Music

First Look

Cover or heading

   Title of music sheet

   Date created

   Is there a cover page or an image?

Based on what you already know, what message do you think is portrayed by this image? Are people, symbols, or words used?

The Lyrics

Read the lyrics. White a three-sentence summary describing the main idea of the song.

Choose two phrases of lyrics that caught your attention. Why did they?

   1.

   2.

From Eastern Illinois University Teaching with Primary Sources (www.eiu.edu/~eiutps/), 2009. Reprinted with permission in *Abraham Lincoln and His Era: Using the American Memory Project to Teach with Primary Sources* by Bobbi Ireland. Santa Barbara, CA: Libraries Unlimited. Copyright © 2010.

Song Purpose

What social or cultural topic is this song about?

Based on the lyrics, what in your opinion seems to be the viewpoint expressed in the song? Why do you think it was written?

Do the images express this viewpoint? How?

At the time this song was written, who might have bought and/or sung this song? How do you think the public reacted to this song?

How can you learn more about the person who wrote this song?

From Eastern Illinois University Teaching with Primary Sources (www.eiu.edu/~eiutps/), 2009. Reprinted with permission in *Abraham Lincoln and His Era: Using the American Memory Project to Teach with Primary Sources* by Bobbi Ireland. Santa Barbara, CA: Libraries Unlimited. Copyright © 2010.

Storyboard

Create a Storyboard to Use Images to Visually Tell a Story.

What is the theme of your storyboard?

Examples: song, place, speech, person, or event

Select images that represent the theme.

- Images can be placed in sequence to reflect a variety of characteristics: time periods, size, geography, etc.
- Select particularly meaningful images to begin and end the storyboard.
- Students may be limited to a specific number of squares.

Image #1   Image #2

$\Rightarrow$

From Eastern Illinois University Teaching with Primary Sources (www.eiu.edu/~eiutps/), 2009. Reprinted with permission in *Abraham Lincoln and His Era: Using the American Memory Project to Teach with Primary Sources* by Bobbi Ireland. Santa Barbara, CA: Libraries Unlimited. Copyright © 2010.

116 Appendix

Image #3

⇒   ⇒

Image #4   Image #5

⇒

From Eastern Illinois University Teaching with Primary Sources (www.eiu.edu/~eiutps/), 2009. Reprinted with permission in *Abraham Lincoln and His Era: Using the American Memory Project to Teach with Primary Sources* by Bobbi Ireland. Santa Barbara, CA: Libraries Unlimited. Copyright © 2010.

Sound Recording

Before Listening

Based on information provided and what you already know . . .

What is the title?

Whose voices will you hear?

When was it created?

While Listening

Type of sound recording (may be more than one):

- Policy speech
- News report
- Entertainment broadcast
- Campaign speech

- Congressional testimony
- Interview
- Other

- Panel discussion
- Court testimony
- Press conference ———

Unique qualities of the recording (may be more than one):

- Music
- Special effects
- Background noise

- Narration
- Live broadcast
- Other———

What is the mood or tone of the recording? How do music, narration, sound effects, and other noises contribute to the *mood* of the recording?

From Eastern Illinois University Teaching with Primary Sources (www.eiu.edu/~eiutps/), 2009. Reprinted with permission in *Abraham Lincoln and His Era: Using the American Memory Project to Teach with Primary Sources* by Bobbi Ireland. Santa Barbara, CA: Libraries Unlimited. Copyright © 2010.

After Listening

Circle speakers that you listed in the previewing activity that were in the recording.

List three things in this sound recording that you think are important.

1.

2.

3.

List two things this recording tells about life in the United States at the time it was made.

1.

2.

What is the central message of this recording?

Was the speaker effective in communicating the message?

Was it more important WHO the speaker was than HOW the speaker communicated?

Who do you think the creators wanted to listen to this recording?

Write a question to the creator that is left unanswered by the recording.

From Eastern Illinois University Teaching with Primary Sources (www.eiu.edu/~eiutps/), 2009. Reprinted with permission in *Abraham Lincoln and His Era: Using the American Memory Project to Teach with Primary Sources* by Bobbi Ireland. Santa Barbara, CA: Libraries Unlimited. Copyright © 2010.

Written Document

First Look

Type of document (check):

- Newspaper
- Map
- Report
- Congressional Record

- Letter
- Telegram
- Memorandum
- Census report

- Patent
- Press release
- Advertisement
- Other———

Unique physical characteristics of the document (check one or more):

- Interesting letterhead
- Typed
- Notations
- Other

- Handwritten
- Seals
- Received stamp
- ———

Date(s) of the document:

Author (or creator) of the document:

    Position (title):

For what audience was the document written?

Document Content Information

List three phrases or statements that caught your attention or that you think are important.

    1.

    2.

From Eastern Illinois University Teaching with Primary Sources (www.eiu.edu/~eiutps/), 2009. Reprinted with permission in *Abraham Lincoln and His Era: Using the American Memory Project to Teach with Primary Sources* by Bobbi Ireland. Santa Barbara, CA: Libraries Unlimited. Copyright © 2010.

Why do you think this document was written?

What in the document helps you know why it was written? Quote from the document.

Why do you think this document was saved?

Was the document meant to be viewed by the public or by a specific person or group?

List two things the document tells you abut life in the Unites States at the time it was written.

　　1.

　　2.

Write a question to the author that is left unanswered by the document.

Photo: ABC

Examine the image. Choose words or phrases that begin with each letter of the alphabet. The words or phrases should come to mind when you look at the image. The words or phrases can be what you see in the image or what the image makes you feel.

A—————————— B——————————

C—————————— D——————————

E—————————— F——————————

G—————————— H——————————

I—————————— J——————————

K—————————— L——————————

M—————————— N——————————

O—————————— P——————————

Q—————————— R——————————

S—————————— T——————————

U—————————— V——————————

W—————————— X——————————

Y—————————— Z——————————

From Eastern Illinois University Teaching with Primary Sources (www.eiu.edu/~eiutps/), 2009. Reprinted with permission in *Abraham Lincoln and His Era: Using the American Memory Project to Teach with Primary Sources* by Bobbi Ireland. Santa Barbara, CA: Libraries Unlimited. Copyright © 2010.

Bibliography

Library of Congress, January 9, 2009, http://www.loc.gov.

Rich, Cynthia. Eastern Illinois University Teaching with Primary Sources. Eastern Illinois University, July 13, 2009, http://www.eiu.edu/~eiutps.

Analysis Tools

Rich, Cynthia. Eastern Illinois University Teaching with Primary Sources. Eastern Illinois University, July 13, 2009, http://www.eiu.edu/~eiutps.

Acknowledgements

Marzano, Robert, and Kendall, John. *Content Knowledge: A Compendium of Standards and Benchmarks for K-12 Education*, 4th ed. Denver, CO: McREL, 2009, http://www.mcrel.org/standards-benchmarks/.

Index

1846, 69, 70
1848, 7, 12, 13
1855, 16
1858, 20, 21, 24, 25, 28, 29
1860, 6, 9, 12, 15, 20, 24, 28, 31, 33, 34, 40, 41, 70, 73, 74, 77
1861, 36, 37, 44, 45, 48, 52, 56, 60, 64, 81, 85, 90, 93
1863, 36, 37, 52, 53, 56, 57
1864, 60, 61
1865, 48, 49, 64, 66, 85, 86, 91

abolish, 9, 10, 11
African American troops, 56, 57
American Memory Collection, 1, 2
assassination of Lincoln, 64, 65, 66, 85, 86, 87, 89

Bedell, Grace, 40, 41
black troops, 56
Butterfield, Justin, 5, 6, 7

cabinet, 33, 60, 62
cartoon analysis, 97
certificate of membership, 73, 74
Civil War, 36, 44, 48, 52, 56, 60, 64, 81, 85, 87, 93
congratulation letters, 32–35
Congress, 1, 11–13, 62, 77
copyright restrictions, 2
curriculum, 2

differentiated instruction, 2
document analysis tools, 11
Douglas, Stephen, 20–22

emancipation, 52, 53, 81–83
Emancipation Proclamation, 52, 53
extension activities, 3

first inaugural address, 44, 45
Ford's Theatre, 85, 86
Fowler, Mrs. Luther, 48, 49
Fry, John B., 33

Grant, Ulysses S., 56, 57
inauguration, 36–38, 46
iron casts, 93

Jones, James W., 33

learning activities, 3
lesson plan, 1, 2, 5, 15, 69
letter analysis, 7, 10, 11
Library of Congress, 1, 2, 7, 16, 21, 25, 29, 33, 37, 38, 41, 45, 49, 53, 57, 61, 65, 70, 74, 78, 82, 86, 90, 94

map analysis, 101
Matie, Julia, 36–39
Medill, Joseph, 24–26
Mexican War, 12–14
military, 56–58
motion picture analysis, 105–106
music sheet analysis, 113

Nast, Thomas, 81–83
national learning standards, 2

painting, 47, 50, 81–83, 85–87
photo analysis, 103, 104, 111
photographs, 1, 77–79, 101
poem, 3, 69, 70–72, 107, 108
poem analysis, 114
popular sovereignty, 28, 29
poster analysis, 74, 89, 90, 94
primary source, 1–3, 5–8, 10, 11, 14, 16, 17, 21, 25, 29, 33, 36, 37, 38, 40–43, 45, 46, 49, 52–54, 56, 57, 61, 62, 65, 69–71, 73, 74, 78, 82, 83, 86, 90, 94

railroads, 6–8
reward posters, 89–91
rubric, 1, 15, 18, 19, 23, 27, 30, 31, 34, 35, 39, 43, 47, 51, 55, 59, 63, 67, 72, 76, 80, 84, 88, 92

secondary source, 1
Senate, 15, 16, 17, 18, 25
slave, 1, 10, 48–50, 57, 58, 81, 83
slave owners, 49
sound recording analysis, 117
speech, 3, 8, 11, 12, 13, 14, 28, 29, 30, 46, 54, 115
Speed, Joshua F., 33
storyboard, 115

Washburne, Elihu B., 15–17
written document analysis, 7, 10, 11, 13, 119

About the Author

BOBBI IRELAND grew up in Illinois and loved hearing stories about Abraham Lincoln. He walked on land not far from where she grew up and would make frequent stops in a neighboring town to visit a pub on his travels through the area.

It wasn't until the summer of 2008 when she was chosen to participate in the Learning with Lincoln Institute at Eastern Illinois University that she really became interested in primary sources and using them to teach about Abraham Lincoln and other historical events.

Bobbi has a degree in early childhood education from Eastern Illinois University and teaching certificates in early childhood education, elementary education, and special education. She presently teaches preschool in Illinois and is a freelance writer. Bobbi is married to John and has two sons, Cameron and Preston.

www.ingramcontent.com/pod-product-compliance
Lightning Source LLC
Chambersburg PA
CBHW080940300426
44115CB00017B/2892